D0600591

AMERICA'S
MYSTERIOUS
PLACES

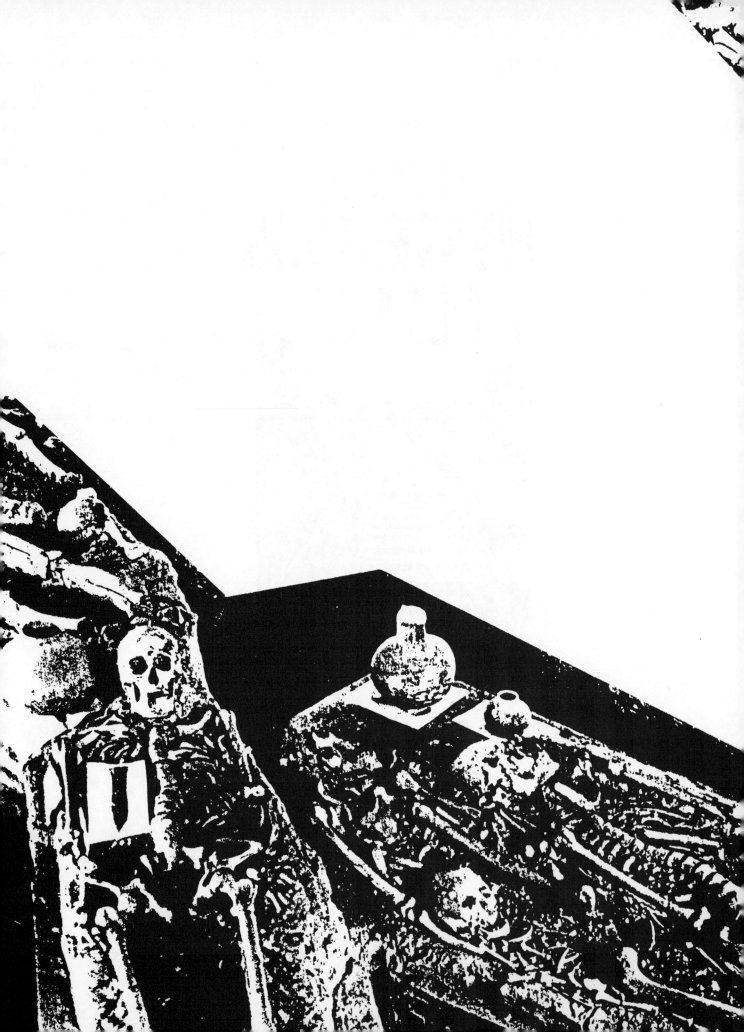

AMERICA'S
MYSTERIOUS
PLACES

Hans Holzer

LONGMEADOW
PRESS

ACKNOWLEDGMENTS

I would like to thank the Departments of Tourism of the Commerce Departments, of the following States for their cooperation: Arizona, Arkansas, California, Connecticut, Florida, Georgia, Iowa, Kentucky, Maine, Maryland, Massachusetts, Michigan, Minnesota, Mississippi, Montana, Nebraska, Nevada, New Hampshire, New Jersey, New Mexico, North Carolina, Ohio, Oklahoma, Pennsylvania, Rhode Island, South Carolina, Tennessee, Vermont, Virginia, Washington, West Virginia, and Wyoming.

I am indebted to Karl P. Stofko, DDS, the Municipal Historian of East Haddam, Connecticut, for his help with the material regarding Moodus, which now forms part of East Haddam.

Copyright © 1992 by Hans Holzer

Published by Longmeadow Press, 201 High Ridge Road, Stamford, CT 06904. All rights reserved. No part of this book may be reproduced or utilized in any form or by any means, electronic or mechanical, including photocopying, recording or by any information storage and retrieval system, without permission in writing from the Publisher.

Cover design by Allan Mogel
Interior design by Allan Mogel

Library of Congress Cataloging-in-Publication Data
Holzer, Hans, 1920–
    America's mysterious places / by Hans Holzer.—1st ed.
       p.   cm.
    ISBN 0-681-41571-1
    1. United States—History, Local—Anecdotes.   2. Curiosities and wonders—United States—Anecdotes.   3. Historic sites—United States—Guidebooks.   4. United States—Guidebooks.   I. Title.
E180.H86   1992
917.304′928—dc20   92-15894
                                                                                 CIP

ISBN: 0-681-41571-1
Printed in United States of America
First Edition
0 9 8 7 6 5 4 3 2 1

INTRODUCTION

What exactly is a "mysterious place," you may ask? A mystery, to begin with, is a situation, event, or location, where some information, some element concerning it, is not fully resolved or clear. A mystery leaves room for further exploration, further investigation and research. It also leaves room for further speculation.

We know very little about the world we live in, and despite advances in technology and communications, there remain many unanswered questions. Throughout America there are many such puzzles. In most cases, no official efforts are being made to solve a given mystery. Sometimes it is not even acknowledged as such. It is relegated instead into the safe and often preferred category of tradition, legend, or hearsay.

I have attempted to carefully select a number of such places widely scattered throughout the United States, without any claim to either completeness or scale of importance.

There are, in essence, three kinds of "mysterious places" found in this work.

1. Naturally-formed places, where unusual, strange or otherwise puzzling formations or events exist or have existed. These contain elements of mystery not created by man.

2. Ordinary places, where extraordinary events have been observed, such as religious shrines, miracle sites, or sites alleged to have unusual powers.

3. Sites where events have occurred in the past, such as battle-grounds or historical events. A sensitive person might relive or sense the "living vibrations" of past happenings. Included here might be verified, authenticated hauntings.

To the best of my knowledge, all of the places herein mentioned can be visited. Whenever I felt it helpful, I have given directions, or mentioned nearby major cities.

It may come as a surprise to many that the U.S. contains so

many interesting and unusual places. Tourist and travel agencies, whether private or governmental, tend to publicize major, well-known tourist attractions. This book will add many new travel goals and attractions which are not known to the general public. A better perspective of our historical development may also result from studying this book. The reader will become perhaps more familiar with the Europeans who came here and established their settlements, out of which ultimately developed our present-day civilization and culture. Thoughtful readers, however, will also realize that these European colonists did not come into a country devoid of culture, but one which already had a civilization of its own. Much of that civilization fell victim to the colonists, who felt obliged to impose their new ways on people who were perfectly happy with their own.

I further wish to express my appreciation to the many local administrators and custodians of sites who helped me with photographs, and to the various historical societies throughout the United States who supplied me with free information and an occasional photograph.

Prof. Hans Holzer, Ph.D.

CONTENTS

AMERICA'S
MYSTERIOUS
PLACES

ARIZONA

THE NAVAJO RESERVATION CANYONS

Located in the middle of the state, the Canyon De Chelly is an area where three great canyons rise up to a height of one thousand feet. There are many pre-historic relics in this area.

For instance, Mummy Cave dates back to 348 A.D., and is in an excellent state of preservation. It consists of two large caves joined by a narrow, hundred-foot long ledge. There are ninety rooms and three *kivas,* or public rooms. Mummy Cave was home to the Basket Makers among the native American tribes until about 1284 A.D. when it seems to have been abandoned. Later the Pueblo Indians moved in and built their homes over the ancient ruins.

The Casa Blanca, or White House, is another spectacular ruin resting on a ledge and dating back to 1066 A.D. It got its name from the white clay covering parts of the walls. This building was constructed the very same year that William the Norman conquered England. The England he found was primitive, torn by petty wars among Saxons and Britons. At the same time, native Americans were erecting sophisticated houses and assembly halls here in Canyon De Chelly.

Photographs Courtesy of the Arizona Office of Tourism

THE PETROGLYPHS OF PHOENIX

South of Phoenix, in what is now called the Hieroglyphic Canyon, there are puzzling drawings on the ancient walls. Puzzling because they do not seem to fit into any tribal pattern known to researchers, and they remain classified as "of uncertain origin."

These drawings are unquestionably extremely ancient and bear a strange resemblance to cave drawings found in France and even to rock drawings in central West Africa. Perhaps they are the work of some pre-historic native tribe of whom we know nothing. Or perhaps they are not of "Indian" origin at all.

Many researchers have come to the conclusion that Europeans and people from Asia Minor and Africa arrived in the Americas long before the Christian era. There are even those who suggest that both these petroglyphs and their European and African "cousins" are the result of an extra-terrestrial landing long ago. Be this as it may, these particular drawings are totally dissimilar from the "usual" native-American rock drawings found elsewhere. They may represent an alphabet used by a people who came here from somewhere else, a people possessed with a higher degree of culture and advanced civilization than those who followed them much later.

Photo Courtesy of the Arizona Office of Tourism

ARKANSAS

FORT SMITH AND THE "HANGING JUDGE"

If it weren't for the reputation of Judge Isaac C. Parker, called the "Hanging Judge", Fort Smith would be an interesting but otherwise unremarkable frontier fortification. Built in 1818 on a lonely and isolated spot, the fort was the starting point of California travellers during the Gold Rush days of the mid 1800s. The U.S. Army abandoned Fort Smith in 1824 due to changes in the boundaries of the Arkansas Territory. It was not until 1838 that a new Fort Smith came into existence on the same spot, mainly to stem the lawlessness that had lately become rampant in the area.

One of the most outspoken advocates of law and order was Judge Parker, who arrived in 1875 ostensibly to restore order in what by then had become a lawless frontier. Outlaws had their way and Indians were often mistreated by the white settlers. Judge Parker had a keen eye out for justice in respect to the native Americans, and he administered the law totally without bias.

His soubriquet of the "Hanging Judge" is not fully justified, however. During his twenty-one years as judge at Fort Smith, he condemned 160 men to death, but only 79 were actually hanged. "It was not I who hung them," Parker said, "It is the law."

The gallows and courtroom are in excellent condition and can be visited. You may even get a feeling of the intense drama that transpired here, if you have that "gift."

Photographs Courtesy of the Fort Smith National Historical Site, National Park Service

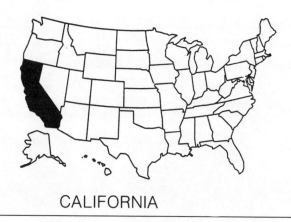

CALIFORNIA

THE MOST HAUNTED HOUSE IN AMERICA

Thanks to the curator, June Reading, and her many volunteer guides and observers, there is a very accurate record of all the strange and mysterious phenomena that have for years been recorded in the Whaley House, built in 1857.

The two-story house was built in Old Town, that part of San Diego considered to be the original section, by Thomas Whaley on the corner of San Diego Avenue and Harney Street.

The house, which is open to visitors, has period furniture throughout—a parlor, a music room, and a library downstairs, and four bedrooms upstairs. In an annex to the left of the main entrance is what was once used as a courtroom.

The sightings by the various guides, and even by some of the visitors, have included a woman in the former courtroom, a man in a frock coat and pantaloons standing at the top of the stairs leading to the upper story, and even a ghost dog scurrying down the hall. Witnesses testify to footfalls galore, doors opening and upstairs windows opening by unseen hands, and the setting off of

Photographs by Doreen Turner and Courtesy of The Whaley House Museum

burglar alarms which could only be tripped by someone *inside* the house when the house was definitely empty. . . . these are the phenomena that went on and are still going on. I held a séance with medium Sybil Leek, with TV host Regis Philbin as my associate, in which the great late medium spoke of one Anna Lanney as one of the earthbound spirits. Anna Lanney was Thomas Whaley's wife. And thereby hangs the ghostly tale: Whaley had a contract with the city of San Diego that the city breached. Having put a lot of money into alterations in the building so the city could use it as a courthouse, he was left "holding the bag", so to speak, and in great anger seemed to have stayed on . . . beyond death.

One of the regular guides, Doreen Turner, has taken photographs from time to time inside the house. In some of them, white shapes appear in what are considered the most active locations— the kitchen downstairs and one of the bedrooms upstairs.

THE BRIDE OF NOB HILL

Nob Hill in San Francisco is a steep elevation leading up to the Fairmount Hotel. It is a busy section of town, with California Street as its central artery. A cable car runs up and down the street and a visitor is likely to encounter all sorts of people walking the street.

A beautiful young woman in a wedding gown has been observed here walking as if trying to get her bearings. Mrs. Gwen Hinzie, who is psychic, saw her walking up California Street in plain daylight in 1962. Others have seen the bride, and seen her walk right *through* flesh-and-blood people!

The woman is thought to be Flora Sommerton, an 18-year-old debutante at the time she was to be married in 1876. But she got cold feet and ran away from home a few hours before her wedding. She never returned, and after a few years, her socially-prominent parents gave up the search. Flora died broke and alone in 1926 in a flophouse hotel in Butte, Montana. When found, she was dressed in the identical white wedding gown she had worn when running away, the same gown people have seen her ghost wear on Nob Hill.

Photos by Hans Holzer

11

THE RUSSIANS IN CALIFORNIA

Most Americans know that Alaska once belonged to Imperial Russia and was purchased from them in 1867, largely through the efforts of then Secretary of State William Seward. But many may not realize that California, too, was influenced by Russia, halfway into the last century.

At Fort Ross, in 1822, on the Pacific coast near Santa Rosa, the Russians had their main outpost. But in 1841 they sold it to John Sutter, the Swiss adventurer. However, the Russian commandant's house, two military blockhouses built by the Russians, and a Russian-Orthodox chapel can still be visited.

What is intriguing about these buildings is their obvious purpose of establishing a permanent Imperial Russian presence in California, at a time when California had barely shaken off its Spanish colonial status which ended in 1822. The United States government's ownership of the territory thus was by no means assured.

The blockhouses are solidly constructed as if to resist military attacks. The Russian-Orthodox chapel with its icons and gold and silver ornaments, its candles and saints, was not a church serving an exile community as are similar chapels in New York and other cities with large Russian emigre populations— but a chapel meant to serve *Russian Californians!*

By 1840, the Russian government lost interest in this expansion of the Empire, perhaps because of mounting political unrest at home.

Photo Courtesy of the California Office of Tourism

THE WINCHESTER HOUSE

Winchester is a little town near Palm Springs which has no particular attraction except for a strange house that has become, over the years, a must see for those visiting the area.

The house itself is a crazy-quilt of annexes and additions, none of which make any real sense in terms of architecture or needs.

The owner and sole inhabitant of this house was a lady who had somehow become convinced that she would not die as long as she kept adding new sections to her house. So she kept doing just that, and in time ran out of logical needs.

This woman had an incredible fear of death and she spent a good deal of her money seeking ways of cheating death. A psychic told her that as long as she kept adding to her house, she would not die. Whether the psychic meant it seriously or as a joke, the woman took it seriously enough to follow it, year after year, keeping to herself and avoiding contacts with the outside world as much as possible. Eventually, of course, death caught up with her.

Photo Courtesy of the California Office of Tourism

AETNA SPRINGS

Aetna Springs is a little-known resort spot near St. Helena, in northern California, above San Francisco. It is an old-fashioned place frequented over the years mainly by older people. It has a good-size golf course.

In 1963, a San Francisco-based physician, Dr. Andrew von Salza, went to Aetna Springs for a brief vacation. The doctor was a camera buff and got to talking with the owner of the resort, George Heibel, who owned a stereo camera which, at the time, was the latest thing in photography. Von Salza asked to borrow it and take some pictures in stereo, and the owner agreed. It was midafternoon on a sunny day when the doctor took several shots with this camera, out on the golf course. Two of the shots, later developed, showed something neither man had counted on—robed monks, enveloped by flames, walking on the empty golf course! Heibel was shocked and immediately assumed the devil was playing tricks with his camera, so he gave it to the doctor as a gift.

When I visited the place with medium Sybil Leek some years later, she spoke, in trance, of a group of monks being persecuted by another group of monks. Sybil had not seen the pictures nor been told of their existence. She also spoke of the leader of this group of monks who had been done to death here, as being named Hieronymus.

On my return to San Francisco and Los Angeles, I tried, in vain, to find evidence that a mission had existed there. All the historical societies assured me there were never any missions or even settlements by monks in this area.

But I could not rest until I knew the story behind the Aetna Springs mystery. In New York I went through the files and storage bins of the Hispanic Society Museum, and there I found the answer.

In a Spanish broadside, a printed document not unlike a

Photos by Dr. Andrew von Salza

newspaper, dated 1532, the world was informed that a group of rebellious Franciscans had caused trouble way up north in California. They had found that the Spaniards were abusing the native American laborers in the silver mines of the area, and they complained about it to the Spanish Crown in Madrid. Far from being sympathetic to the injustices visited upon the poor Indians, the Spanish government alerted the Dominican Friars in San Francisco to look into the matter. The Dominicans were associated with the dreaded Inquisition in Europe. And, sure enough, the Dominicans came and burned the Franciscans for their "rebellion." And the leader of the Franciscans was named Hieronymus.

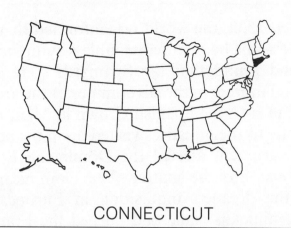

CONNECTICUT

THE CURSE OF THE DUDLEYS

About two hours' drive north from New York City, in Litchfield County, is what was once a real town—Dudleytown. Now it is only a ghost town, and according to the late medium Ethel Johnson Myers, who lived nearby and visited it often, there are some real ghosts there.

Overlooking the village of Cornwall Bridge, Indians used to hunt in the hills, and owls, lots of them, lived in the oak and chestnut trees. It was from them that the village acquired the nickname of Owlsbury.

In the middle of the 1800s, English colonists had moved into the area, among them the brothers Abiel and Barzillai Dudley. The Dudleys farmed the land and prospered and soon the town acquired their name—Dudleytown. But the good fortunes of family and town were not to last. Gradually, settlers moved away, houses crumbled, and the area seemed to want to return to its original condition prior to the arrival of the English. It did not seem possible that all this good fortune should end so tragically. By the turn of the century, the town had become a ghost town. There is no *rational explanation* for this flight from the gentle hills of Connecticut by everyone who came to live there. The real reason for Dudleytown's fate lies elsewhere.

The first Dudleys had put an ocean between themselves and their past, so perhaps they assumed they were safe from the terrible *curse of the Dudleys!*

The Dudleys had angered the Tudor monarchs of England by siding with the rebels who attempted to place Lady Jane Grey on the throne. Both Lady Jane and her mentor, Lord Guilford Dudley, were executed as soon as Bloody Mary became queen. His brother fell out of favor with the next queen, Mary's half sister Elizabeth I. He was forced to flee for his life abroad. It was his direct descendant, William Dudley, who founded what eventually became known as Dudleytown. They say the curse of the Tudors came along with him to America.

Not only did it wipe out the Dudleys, it also did in any others who might want to live in the accursed place—the Carters, the Greeleys, and its last inhabitant, William C. Clark, M.D. He had bought the ghost town in 1910 as an investment, hoping to develop the area, and defying the curse. Then his wife went stark, raving mad, for no apparent reason. That was enough for Dr. Clark: he locked up the last house, and left, never to return. That was some eighty years ago, and the place has been empty ever since. . . . except for the ghosts.

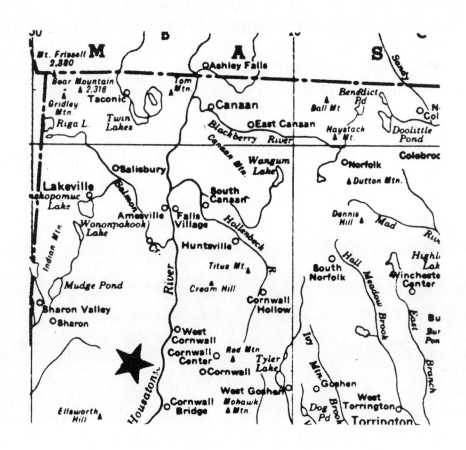

THE MOODUS NOISES

Moodus is a village in the town of East Haddam, and consists of a small shopping center, a twine mill, and a small green surrounded by a few old houses, a church, a library, and a school. The name "Moodus" comes from the native "Place of Bad Noises" or Matchemadoset, which eventually developed into Machimoodus, or Moodus for short.

What makes this place interesting are noises that seemingly emanate from below the surface of the earth. These rumbling, menacing sounds have puzzled people in the area back to the native Indians. The natives attributed the rumblings and earth tremors which accompany them to the god Hobomoko, who sat below on his sapphire throne and ruled over humanity.

The disturbances center around Mount Tom and a nearby cave, said to be the entrance to the god's realm. Modern seismologists consider the disturbances to be caused by earth tremors in the fault lines in the area.

Photos Courtesy of Dr. Karl P. Stofko

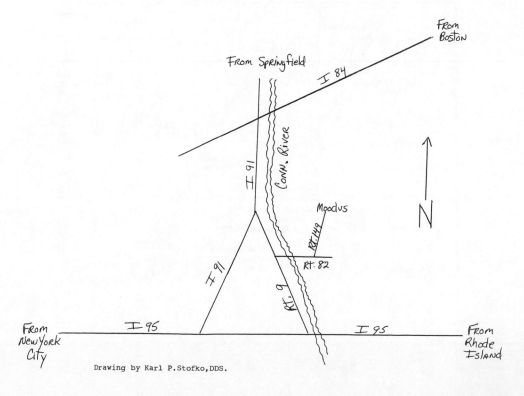

Drawing by Karl P. Stofko, DDS.

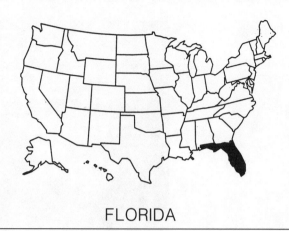

FLORIDA

THE GAMBLE PLANTATION

This mansion, built between 1842 and 1845, would be yet another example of the Greek-revival style in the South, except for the fact that it was the last refuge for a man who had played an important role in the Civil War.

The man was Judah P. Benjamin, Secretary of State to Jefferson Davis, and also a pillar of the Jewish community in the South. When the Confederate cause was lost, Benjamin came here to hide. The Union government had every reason to want to bring him to trial and eventually execute him. It was Judah P. Benjamin, the wealthy banker, who single-handedly helped finance the Confederacy by persuading other wealthy people to contribute to the cause.

Benjamin thought that hiding away from his Union pursuers as long as possible might spare his life, since the passions would eventually die down. He was right. Hiding out in one of the more obscure plantations in the South, his chances of being discovered were small. He knew he could trust his host. Gamble Plantation was not the refuge one would expect the Secretary of State of the Confederacy to choose! Ellenton is in Sarasota County and is open to visitors.

Photo by H. Milo Stewart III, Courtesy of the Florida Department of Commerce, Division of Tourism

FORT JEFFERSON

About 70 miles west of Key West are the small islands known as the Dry Tortugas. Today, they are a wildlife paradise. In the eighteenth century, pirates and smugglers stayed there because the place was so difficult to reach from the mainland.

One of the Dry Tortugas boasts a ruin of a very large fortification called Fort Jefferson. Today, it is an empty shell. Half a mile around, this huge fortress is also surrounded by a deep moat. Getting out of the Fort wasn't at all easy—sort of an American Devil's Island.

Dr. Samuel Mudd became a convicted criminal for the sole humanitarian act of setting John Wilkes Booth's broken ankle! He had nothing to do with the assassination of Abraham Lincoln, and defended his action as something he would have done for anyone, the devil himself, if he came looking for help. But Mudd was sent to Fort Jefferson and spent most of his life in the island prison. No doubt his anguish must still cling to the walls of his cell.

His great-grandson has been petitioning the United States government to set the unjust conviction of his ancestor aside.

Photos Courtesy of the Florida Department of Commerce, Division of Tourism

FORT MATANZAS

Measuring only thirty by forty feet, Fort Matanzas in St. Augustine would hardly deserve to be noted, except for a terrible crime committed here. Built in 1737, the fort was a secondary fortification of the oldest Spanish settlement, St. Augustine. The spot where it stands witnessed the *massacre* of French settlers who had claimed Florida for France in 1565.

The French settlers had escaped from France because they were persecuted by Catholics. These Protestants (Huguenots) had come face to face with the ever-increasing and ruthless power of the Spanish conquistadores. General Menendez, the regional commandant, invited them to discuss problems of co-existence, or so he claimed. When they showed up in good faith, he had them massacered by his troops. To Menendez, killing "heretics" served two ends—the Catholic Church and the Spanish Crown.

As a result of this treachery by Menendez, Florida became a Spanish possession. A sensitive person may well feel the anguish of this long-ago event while visiting the spot. It is not likely to have faded away completely over the centuries.

Photo by H. Milo Stewart III, Courtesy of the Florida Department of Commerce, Division of Tourism.

HENRY FLAGLER'S MANSION

Henry Flagler was Florida's greatest booster, although the eccentric millionaire didn't always please everyone.

He made his money in grain and oil (as Rockefeller's partner), and recently widowed, moved from Cleveland to New York with his small son. Shortly after, he married his wife's nurse, Alice.

About that time Flagler discovered St. Augustine on a vacation trip and decided to go into the hotel business, first with the Ponce de Leon Hotel in St. Augustine, and later with the Royal Poinciana in Palm Beach. He "created" St. Augustine, making it into a fashionable resort, and he did the same for Palm Beach. Alice became ill and was confined to a mental institution.

In 1895, Henry Flagler went to work to "create" Miami. With Alice out of the way, Flagler met a young singer named Mary Kenan. But both father and his son, now grown, were in love with Mary, and it destroyed their relationship. Henry divorced his wife even though she was institutionalized. He bribed the Florida Legislature to pass a special law to make it possible for him to marry Mary Kenan, which he did.

The outraged people of Florida forced Henry to leave the state. He lived with Mary in suburban New York, but the call of Florida was too strong to resist.

He decided to return there, and to regain his lost popularity with the people of Florida, Henry decided on something spectacular. He built a railroad connecting the mainland with the keys. This railroad extended all the way to Key West. At age 82, Henry was once more a hero. But some thirty years later, after his death, a raging storm washed his railroad right into the sea. Today there is no railroad, but there is a causeway where it used to run.

Photo Courtesy of the Florida Department of Commerce, Division of Tourism

Whitehall, the magnificent mansion Flagler lived in in Palm Beach, is now a museum.

But if you go up to the top floor, under the roof, perhaps you may catch a glimpse of Henry himself. I hear he never really left.

GEORGIA

ANDERSONVILLE, A CIVIL WAR HORROR CAMP

No war is more savagely fought than a civil war. History never changes in this respect—from Octavian's war against the Caesar murderers in ancient Rome, through the Thirty Years' War of Catholics against Protestants, in the 16th century, to Spain's Civil War and the current violence in what was Yugoslavia.

In America, the War Between the States turned ordinary citizens into angry, cruel people, who would kill or mistreat a fellow American only because he wore the wrong color uniform.

So it was that the Confederate prison camp at Andersonville, under Swiss-born James Wirth, became a deathtrap. The sadistic commandant treated captured Yankee soldiers in such a way that over 52,000 perished there. Lack of food and medicine was the principal cause of their deaths. Many are buried in the Andersonville cemetary.

While Andersonville does not quite match the horror of the Nazi concentration camps, for its time it was the depth of cruelty. It seemed all the worse since it pitted countryman against countryman.

Andersonville is due southeast of Columbus, and the burial ground still elicits strong emotions.

Photograph Courtesy of the Tourist Division, Georgia Department of Industry and Trade

GEORGIA'S PREFERRED CAPITAL

Everybody knows that Atlanta is the capital of the Peachtree State. But that was not always the case. When Atlanta was still known as Terminus (from the railroad terminus located there), Georgians looked with pride to another city, more centrally located, called Milledgeville. Allegedly, the site was chosen on the advice of a mystic who claimed Milledgeville was a "sacred site."

In 1838 Milledgeville was made the state capital, and an appropriate executive mansion had to be erected. But very few Georgians knew the real reason behind *that selection,* and probably don't to this day. After some discussion the powers that be chose the justly famous Palladio mansions of Europe as their model, and the same year the Executive Mansion was built in a style Palladio himself could not have bettered.

Milledgeville to this day is a medium-size city with two hospitals, due south of Atlanta. From 1838–1868, Georgia's center was here—right through the Civil War. Atlanta was burned by the Union troops, but Milledgeville escaped.

Photo Courtesy of the Tourist Division, Georgia Department of Industry and Trade

BURR'S REFUGE ON ST. SIMON'S ISLAND

In 1736, James Oglethorpe, the founder of the colony of Georgia, decided to build a fort on St. Simon's Island. Fort Frederica would protect the English colony from Spanish forces. Toward the north end of the island was Major Pierce Butler's plantation. The ruins of the house can be visited today. It was in this house that Aaron Burr took refuge after killing Alexander Hamilton in a duel in Weehawken, New Jersey.

The duel came about after years of rivalry between Hamilton and Colonel Burr. Political innuendos and slurs against Burr during the campaign for the governorship of New York finally caused him to challenge Hamilton to a duel.

The duel took place on July 11, 1804, and Hamilton was the loser. The state of New Jersey then indicted Burr for murder. Nominally, duelling was illegal, but this indictment was motivated purely by political reasons. Rather than face arrest, Burr, then Vice President of the United States, fled.

Photo Courtesy of the Tourist Division, Georgia Department of Industry and Trade

THE SOUTH'S OWN MOUNT RUSHMORE

Mount Rushmore National Monument in South Dakota honors four United States presidents and its facade is familiar to nearly every American. Not so with Stone Mountain, Georgia. Located near Atlanta, the huge granite rock served for centuries as a signal tower for native Americans. The Cherokees used the top of the rock to send smoke signals to their people and tribes allied with them.

After the War Between the States, the South wanted to honor those who led their fight, even though they had failed. The result was a rock carving which is the world's largest work of sculptural art.

It depicts Jefferson Davis, Robert E. Lee and Thomas "Stonewall" Jackson riding into the Georgia sunset. These men were chosen because they were, to Southerners, the true heroes of the Civil War.

Photo Courtesy of the Tourist Division, Georgia Department of Industry and Trade

IOWA

THE CURIOUS EFFIGY MOUNDS OF MARQUETTE

Iowa is usually praised for its corn, and for the healthy, midwestern population that grows so much of it. But it has its fair share of interesting historical sites. In the little town of Marquette, in northeastern Iowa (on the bluffs facing Wisconsin across the Mississippi River), we find the Effigy Mounds National Monument.

This eloquent testimony to the religious culture of the Hopewell Indians contains over one hundred burial mounds, dating back to 1000 A.D. What makes these particular mounds different from the many native American burial sites throughout the country is the fact that they are in the shape of animals and birds!

There is a Great Bear mound, and a Marching Bear mound, both alluding to the colorful names used by the nature-bound people of this region.

We really know relatively little about the Hopewell Indians. Even the name itself may be only a reference to a place where they lived at one time. While most Indian burial mounds are round and functional, these mounds in animal shape refer to the name or names of Indians buried in them—not unlike Egyptian tombs showing the effigy of the deceased! Could there be a connection? Where did the "Hopewell" Indians come from originally? It is still a mystery.

Photos Courtesy of the Iowa Division of Tourism

KENTUCKY

THE WICKLIFFE MOUNDS

At the Wickliffe Mounds, the Indian artifacts play an exciting and active role in the interpretation of Kentucky's prehistoric heritage.

The site was built by Indians of the Mississippian period, which lasted from about 800 to 1360 A.D. It lies above the confluence of the Ohio and Mississippi rivers and was a ceremonial center where tribes gathered from other areas to worship together; Wickliffe was a site transcending individual tribal boundaries, and sacred to all of them. Traders from a vast area of the eastern United States also gathered here.

Archaeological excavations were conducted here in the 1930s, and *numerous artifacts* were found that *yield clues to the lifestyle of these prehistoric people.* These include weapons, beads, and crude rock drawings. Murrary State University now operates the site as a museum and research center.

Photos Courtesy of the Kentucky Department of Travel Development

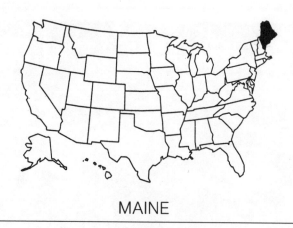

MAINE

A SCOTSMAN'S CASTLE IN AMERICA

In 1807, when Silas Lee decided to build his "castle" in the new world, he wanted it to look like the Greathouses in Scotland. The idea was to transplant as much of the old country to America as possible, including of course any family spirits who cared to travel. Celtic lore supposes that ghosts prefer to be in familiar surroundings, even if it's 3,000 miles away from their native habitat!

The result was a splendid, if somewhat unusual, house boasting a magnificent elliptical staircase. Later, the house passed into the hands of Capt. Richard Tucker who added some Victorian touches to it in 1859. Today the house is known as Castle Tucker or Tucker Mansion, in the town of Wiscasset, in Lincoln County, Maine.

Wiscasset is a gracious seaport, once the favorite of sea captains and those connected with the now defunct clipper ships; an important town, too, for the merchants of the time.

Photo Courtesy of the Maine Historic Preservation Commission

THE OLDEST JAIL IN NEW ENGLAND

York is the site of The Old Gaol, probably the oldest jail in New England that remains in its original shape and condition. It is located in York Village, Maine.

Built in 1720 and added on to up to 1806, it even has a dungeon. If you were to stand in it, you might experience some of its past events, if you are sensitive to the vibrations clinging to its ancient masonry.

In 1879, the jail was abandoned as a prison and in the 1890s it served as a schoolhouse.

Nobody knows who built the Old Gaol—there are two cells for prisoners, and facilities for the prison guards who lived at the jail. In colonial parlance, this was referred to as a "house of correction", though one wonders how much correcting the Old Gaol did for its unfortunate inmates.

Photo Courtesy of the Maine Historic Preservation Commission

THE WEDDING-CAKE HOUSE

This unique house was built in the Gothic Revival style for George W. Bourne in 1826. He could well afford it, for he was a partner in the prosperous shipbuilding firm of Bourne and Kingsbury. Their yards were right on the Kennebunk River where many clipper ships and other vessels originated during the nineteenth century. The Kennebunk River area was indeed prosperous beyond belief.

Mr. Bourne wanted something very special for a home, and did not care about the cost.

No other house in Maine or, for that matter, New England is even remotely similar. The elaborate style simply was never indiginous to the area. But then the "Wedding-Cake House", as it came to be called because of its elaborate trim, was not designed by an architect, but by a shipbuilder! To him, the fancy trim on the house was like "the icing on a wedding cake."

The house looks more like a fancy ship than a house on firm land. That is of course intentional—to a shipbuilder or owner, living in a "land ship" may transfer the good fortunes of the sea-going vessel to the house.

Photograph Courtesy of the Maine Historic Preservation Commission

MARYLAND

THE *CONSTELLATION*, SHIP OF DESTINY

Fully restored to its former glory, the proud frigate *Constellation,* a major tourist attraction, lies in Baltimore harbor. It had taken years of restoration to bring the ship, which had fallen into disrepair, back into shape.

Built in 1798, the frigate went to work guarding American merchant shipping against piracy. Under the command of Captain Thomas Truxton, she became America's *"ship of destiny."* After seeing action in the War of 1812, and in other engagements, she was briefly retired. But then she returned to active service during the War Between the States.

Eventually the ship showed her age, and by 1953 the *Constellation* was in very poor condition. The people of Baltimore raised the funds to restore her. The restoration committee was less than enthusiastic at the reports of hauntings aboard. They feared it might deter visitors from coming aboard, but fortunately quite the opposite turned out to be true.

Even while the ship was undergoing repairs, strange events

Photo Courtesy of the Baltimore Restoration Committee

took place. On July 26, 1959, a priest came aboard and walked around by himself, since the curator was too busy at the time. But the priest said he did not mind. After all, the old gent had shown him around!

What old gent, the curator wanted to know. The priest explained that he had been greeted by an old man in naval uniform who apparently knew his way around the ship. Of course, no such naval officer had been aboard at the time.

The curator investigated the matter and discovered that similar incidents had happened wherever the ship had berthed through the years. The wheel had been seen spinning seemingly by itself. A Navy Commander had seen "a man in an early uniform" walking the quarter deck at night. An old sailor smiled at a lady visitor seated on a bench and then disolved into thin air.

When the late medium Sybil Leek was brought in and went below deck and into trance, she was able to identify one ghost as Captain Truxton by name—even though she had no knowledge of his identity or name. She also identified a sailor who had been executed during the war against the French, because he had fallen asleep at his post. Sybil even got his name right, speaking of someone named "Harsen" or something similar. The sailor's name had actually been Neil *Harvey*.

If you visit the *Constellation,* there are guides around. Of course, if one of them is dressed in an earlier uniform, better say a polite hello to the good Captain Truxton, or the unfortunate Harvey.

FOLLINS POND

Follins Pond is today a quiet inland lake on Cape Cod, halfway between Cape Cod Bay and Nantucket Sound. It can easily be found by taking Route 6 which runs through the middle of the Cape. During the early Middle Ages, Follins Pond was not a pond at all, but an open inlet which ships could go into from the open ocean. It is here that the Vikings had their first landfall in North America.

That the Norsemen came to America is now common knowledge, and signs in the area speak of "Viking Rock".

In various parts of New England and Canada, remnants of Viking visitations have been found, but it was not until 1967 that actual hard evidence had turned up. A stone found near Byfield, Massachusetts was deciphered and proved Viking presence in the area as of November 24, 1009 A.D.! Other authenticated stones were found as far west as Oklahoma, dated November 11, 1012, and some dated 1015 and 1022.

The traditional date for Leif Ericsson's arrival in America is 1003. Ericsson, in his chronicles, had described an "offshore island" in the area of the Cape. Explorer and author Frederick Pohl thought that it was actually not an island but part of the

Photo by Hans Holzer

50

Cape itself that was occasionally cut off from Nantucket by high tides. But Charles Michael Boland, an expert on Viking landings, thought the site of that first landfall was on the Cape, and that the "island" was no island at all, but an inlet of the sea, but where *exactly?*

I decided to try and pinpoint that site with the help of famed psychic Sybil Leek, and I brought her to Follins Pond. Not only did she verify that suspicion (not knowing where she was, or why) but she also spoke, in trance, of a Viking longboat at the bottom of the pond. Her description of the boat and the men she saw from the past, were both convincing and accurate.

Unfortunately, nobody has yet come forward to finance a diving expedition into the pond. We can only hope that the longboat, and the shields decorating its sides, are still buried in the mud of the pond that was once an open inlet when the Vikings first entered it from the sea.

THE OLDEST CHURCH IN NEW ENGLAND

Old Ship Church, begun in 1681, is the sole existing example of a seventeenth century Puritan "meeting house." It is also the oldest church in New England. The Puritans, who had come to the New World after being driven out of England, brought with them their strange and extreme religious customs.

The congregation sat on very uncomfortable wooden benches with narrow seats—men on one side, women on the other. No central altar was used in the Puritan service, and the building was square in shape.

Interestingly, the church was built by ship's carpenters, and cost 420 pounds sterling, or the approximate equivalent of $750,000.00 in today's money. Some enlargements were made in the eighteenth century but the uncomfortable seating arrangements were deliberately kept that way. Puritanism was the result of religious fanaticism by those who essentially denied the comforts of the material world as being sinful. Wealth, sexual pleasures, art and music were all frowned upon.

Located on Main Street, in Hingham, Plymouth County, the church is presently owned by the Unitarians. The design of this building was unique with the Puritans, but no similar structure exists. The new settlers decided to create their own design that would be better suited for a meeting house.

Photo Courtesy of the Massachusettes Historical Commission.

THE SHIP CHANDLER'S GHOST AT COHASSET

S hip chandlers did big business dealing in all kinds of equipment and goods when whaling was in its heyday along the Massachsetts coast. But when the trade fell off, so did business and things were never quite the same.

The solid two-story house at 6 Elm Street in Cohasset, not far from Boston, is now a maritime museum. When it was built in 1760, it was the pride and joy of Samuel Bates, whose family prospered in the ship chandlery business. The house stood at the seashore, long after Samuel had presumably gone to his just reward.

The later owners of the property thought a new location in town would be more conducive to tourist visits. It was decided to move the house to a new location. That was in 1957, and while they were at it, the town decided to fix up some of the old furbishings, such as doors and windows, and replace them with new ones. One would think that all these improvements would please the late Samuel Bates and his descendants.

But all was not well at the "Ship Chandlery and Counting House" as it was formally called once the property was moved inland. Persistent reports of heavy footfalls as if caused by a substantially built man, were being talked about in town, and it was soon clear to one and all in Cohasset that old man Bates wasn't happy.

It came as no particular surprise to anyone in town that the late Bob Kennedy, the celebrated Boston radio personality, brought me to look into the matter at the Chandlery and find out what was going on.

Mrs. E. Stoddard Marsh, who was then the curator, and Robert Frost, her associate, had both heard footsteps at various

Photograph Courtesy of the Massachusetts Historical Commission

times and there was a peculiar cold spot in what used to be Mr. Bates inner office upstairs.

With the help of psychics, both amateur and volunteer, and one professional, Alice McDermott, I was able to establish the cause of the haunting. Samuel Bates, or his ghost, was upset about the house having been moved inland, away from the seashore.

If you visit the house be sure to send some good thoughts to Samuel Bates and explain to them that the Ship Chandlery is no less respected nowadays even if the house stands inland now—after all, the fleet's in, too, and permanently so.

THE SALEM WITCH HOUSE

Let it be said from the outset—just as there were never any "real" witches in Salem, there weren't any in this house. But it did belong to one of the judges of the infamous witchcraft trial at the end of the seventeenth century. It is said that the people accused of what the bigotted Puritans believed to be "witches" were paraded in and out of this house during the trials.

Since so much suffering took place here at 310 Essex Street in Salem, Massachusetts, it is very possible that a sensitive visitor might feel their agony all over again. This is called *psychometry,* or measuring an imprint from the past through one's intuitive processes.

The house was built in 1642 and enlarged in 1674, well in advance of the Salem witchcraft trials twenty years later.

While there are no "real" witches connected with the hysteria that resulted in so many deaths of innocent people, there is nowadays a Wiccan coven and school headquartered in Salem. It is led by Laurie Cabot, who calls herself "the official witch of Salem."

Photo Courtesy of the Massachusetts Historical Commission

MICHIGAN

ARCH ROCK

Near Mackinac City on Mackinac Island, Michigan there is a curious rock formation that suggests almost supernatural origin. A perfect rock arch on high ground, it looks out onto the waters of the Straits of Mackinac—the same Straits explorer John Nicolet visited in 1634 in the hope of finding a passage West.

But to the native people who lived there for many centuries before the arrival of white men, Arch Rock was a sacred place. They could not understand how it could have occurred through natural means because they lacked scientific knowledge. None other than the Great Spirit himself had built it, as a symbol of his strength and as a kind of covenant with his people.

It is a mystic place indeed, even though the rock was most likely created by nature over the centuries.

Photo Courtesy of the Michigan Department of Commerce Travel Bureau.

MINNESOTA

THE PIPESTONE QUARRY PUZZLES

The Pipestone Quarry lies near Highway 75, near Pipestone, Minnesota. The Plains Indians mined this quarry for their ceremonial pipes which are famous beyond the boundaries of their area.

The spot where the quarry is situated is considered a sacred place. According to legend, the quarry was "the center of creation", of divine origin and the original source of all native American peoples. Before 1929, the site was administered by the Dakotas, after that the U.S. government turned it into a national monument. Many Indian tribes got their peace pipe stone from here, because the stone of this quarry was considered particularly sacred. They also consecrated the pipes here with ceremonial dances and tribal councils, during which the newly-blessed pipes were smoked.

One of the seemingly "natural" rocks in the quarry has the shape of an Indian head. Some interesting prehistoric rock carvings, dealing with the mythos of the place, were also found here and now can be seen at the local museum.

To this day all native Americans have the right to quarry the peculiar red stone of this site for their own needs.

Photo Courtesy of the Minnestoa Office of Tourism

THE KENSINGTON RUNE STONE

In 1898, a farmer named Olaf Ohman, found a strange, inscribed stone on his land. He did not call in the local newspapers to proclaim his discovery of a Norse relic. He did not try to sell the stone to the highest bidder. He just let it sit there, not really concerned about its importance or value.

But eventually, in 1907, scholars discovered the rune stone and safeguarded it for further study. The runic inscriptions of the stone were clear enough. Eight Swedes and twenty-two Norsemen had ventured to this part of the world on an expedition. They made camp here in 1362 A.D. One day, when some of them came back from fishing in a nearby lake, they found ten of their people killed, presumably by hostile natives. Being Christians, they implored God to save them from evil.

In a scientific world prone to accept only that which it already knows, or is likely to know, any discovery tending to upset that notion is bound to arouse controversy. So an aura of questionability arose about the Kensington rune stone of Alexandria, Minnesota. Nothing is as destructive to further research on a fascinating object or subject, than doubts expressed about its authenticity, no matter how unsupported the accusations may be.

We know that ancient seafaring people from the Mediterranean area came to the United States and left artifacts here, dating from between 3000 and 1500 B.C. So it does appear that this fourteenth century marker left by the Scandinavians is a bit late.

The stone can now be seen in a local museum at Alexandria, near the village of Kensington, where Olaf found the stone embedded in the roots of an aspen tree.

Photo Courtesy of the Rune Stone Museum, Alexandria.

MISSISSIPPI

THE INCIDENT AT PASCAGOULA

Mississippi is a state not known for unusual or even daring adventures. It is a conservative part of the country. Pascagoula is a small town on the Pascagoula River, also known as "the singing river" because of the noises of birds in the area.

But on October 12, 1973 an incident at Pascagoula occurred that defied anything that ever happened in that sleepy little town.

Two shipyard workers, Charles Hickson, 42, and Calvin Parker, 19, were fishing from an old pier on the west bank of the river at about 7 P.M. when they noticed a strange aircraft about two miles distant. As they looked on in bewilderment, the craft came closer until it hovered a few feet above the water. At this point, three very strange-looking figures emerged from the craft, walking or floating toward the two men.

They took Hickson and Parker and carried them aboard the craft. According to the two men, they were kept aboard for about twenty minutes, after which they were brought back to where the

Photo Courtesy of the Jackson County Area Chamber of Commerce

strangers had picked them up, and the craft took off with a flash of light. Hickson and Parker described their abductors as having large eyes and making a buzzing sound. Inside the UFO, the two were looked over by a camera-like instrument, and examined, before being returned to the river.

While this is not so different from other, fully-authenticated abductions by UFOs with similar details, the two men did not have any knowledge of the literature on the subject. Nowadays, they speak about their experience to interested groups, having fully recovered from their shock.

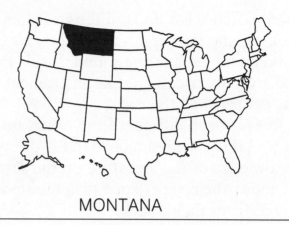

MONTANA

CUSTER'S LAST STAND

One of the great battles of the unfortunate war between native Americans and the United States forces took place on June 25, 1876, near the village of Little Bighorn.

The Seventh Cavalry Regiment, containing six hundred men, was under the command of General George Armstrong Custer. Underestimating the size of the Indian force, he attacked and was wiped out, along with 250 soldiers, by a superior force of Sioux and Cheyenne warriors.

The hill where these men died, and the cemetery nearby where they are buried, is a kind of sacred ground to both Americans and Indians. It reminds them of the folly of war, and it questions the validity of the cause that brought about the death of so many people.

In a way, Custer's Last Stand was also the final stand of the Indian confederates against the United States government, who overcame them in the end and moved them into reservations. The atmosphere here is overpowering and anyone sufficiently sensitive to such vibrations may well re-experience in his or her mind the agony of those hours.

Photo Courtesy of the National Park Service, Department of the Interior

NEBRASKA

CHIMNEY ROCK, STATE SYMBOL

Standing near the town of Bayard, on what used to be the Old Oregon Trail, and sticking out of the surrounding plain, is a unique rock formation. It has served as a Nebraska landmark ever since white settlers came here, and it was an important site for Indians throughout the ages as well. The reason for the special attention awarded to the rock has to do with its uniqueness to the area. No other such rock rises anywhere near it, and no good reason can be found for its existence.

But ancient people have always put almost mystic stock in so-called "markers", believing them to be of divine origin.

The pioneers passing by here on their way westward in the nineteenth century referred to their experience as "seeing the elephant," perhaps because of the gigantic size of the rock, although it looks more like a chimney—therefore the name, Chimney Rock. Rising five hundred feet into the air, the rock is actually a natural marker signalling the end of the plains and the beginning of the Rocky Mountains to the West.

Photo Courtesy of the Nebraska Department of Economic Development

CHIMNEY ROCK
SITE OF THIS HISTORIC LANDMARK OF THE OLD
OREGON TRAIL, MORMON TRAIL, DEADWOOD TRAIL
AND PONY EXPRESS GIVEN TO THE PUBLIC BY
ROSZEL FRANK DURNAL
(1860 - 1939)
TO WHOSE MEMORY
THIS MONUMENT IS GRATEFULLY DEDICATED
WITH RECOGNITION OF PARTICIPATION
OF HIS WIFE MARY B. DURNAL AND CORDIAL
COOPERATION OF HIS FAMILY
ERECTED A.D. 1940
NEBRASKA STATE HISTORICAL SOCIETY

NEBRASKA'S SALUTE TO STONEHENGE

So impressed was visitor Jim Reinders when he saw the ancient dolmens of Stonehenge in Salisbury Plain, England, that he decided to honor them in his own fashion, the American way, back home in Nebraska.

Since he was involved in the automobile business, he decided to build his own version of Stonehenge out of the wrecks of old cars, calling it *Carhenge*.

Carhenge sits on his family farm, on Route 385 in western Nebraska, and even the official tourist agencies, after some initial reluctance, have accepted Jim's "contribution" as a genuine attraction.

While some visitors may smile at the naive attitude that made this used-car dealer put up his own version of Stonehenge, there is something in common with the purpose of the much more famous site in England. Both were meant to be landmarks, set in a conspicous place and both represent their specific culture and beliefs—the ancient Britons' pre-occupation with the deeper meaning of the stars and planets, as guiding their lives, and the modern car dealer's faith in his particular icon of success—the used car.

Photo Courtesy of the Department of Economic Development, Travel and Tourism Division

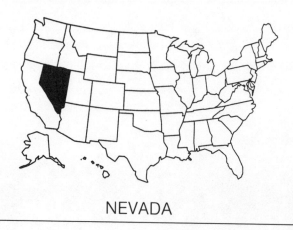

NEVADA

THE VALLEY OF FIRE

North of Las Vegas lies an old native-American hunting ground known as the Valley of Fire. Here, centuries before white men came this way, and before the Pueblo Indians settled here, another race carved strange hieroglyphics into the rocks. These petroglyphs, as they are more properly called, tell the story of the people who once lived in this valley.

Long before Guttenberg invented printing and books came into being, the so-called "savages" of the North American continent had a written language and a need to let those who came after them know about their lives.

This was Nevada's first State Park. It is located fifteen miles from the town of Overton, where there is also a museum. There one can find artifacts found in the Valley, which were the work of the mysterious Anasazi people. The name means "the ancient ones". The tribe disappeared rather suddenly from this area eight hundred years ago, and nobody really knows what happened to them.

Photo Courtesy of Richard F. Moreno of the Nevada Commission on Tourism

THE GHOST TOWN OF RHYOLITE

There are haunted towns, like Dudleytown in Connecticut, and then there are ghost towns, like Rhyolite in Nevada. Sometimes, though, the two types become one.

Overlooking Death Valley, Rhyolite, located four miles from Beatty, flourished in the early years of this century, after gold was discovered there in 1904.

At one time there were three different railroads serving the area. But by 1910 they were all gone because of the disappointing results in the gold fields. By 1920 only fourteen people were left in Rhyolite.

Today, there are unused railroad sidings with the rails still in place, stores long abandoned, houses and places of business. Nothing was removed by wreckers, and no attempt was made to salvage anything of value or sell the rails as scrap metal. The ghost town is stuck in time and so are the emotions that once made this a thriving place of human activity.

Visiting the remnants of what was once a thriving town, with all kinds of amenities, is a strange experience. As elsewhere, those who have "the gift," may just be able to tune in on some remnants of the past, and hear the voices long since stilled.

Photo Courtesy of Richard F. Moreno of the Nevada Commission on Tourism.

THE LIVING VOICES OF VIRGINIA CITY

Virginia City is not only the location of the successful television series, "Bonanza," but a very real historical town. In the 1800s the pioneers, the adventurers searching for gold, the cattle barons, and the badmen of the West met and lived here.

Its once thriving social life is no more, but many of its buildings still stand, carefully preserved. Among them is St. Mary's Church, better known as St. Mary's in-the-Mountains. Built in 1877 at the height of the Comstock Lode mining fever, its bell is made of silver from that lode.

Visitors come to Virginia City all the time, partly because of "Bonanza," and partly out of genuine historical interest. A few years ago a group of curious students of the psychic visited the church to investigate what had been reported by several witnesses.

It seems that the witnesses, who were in no way interested in psychic phenomena, had entered the empty church on a quiet afternoon, only to hear the organ playing music and a far-away sound of garbled voices. But there was no one about, and the organ had long fallen silent.

Photo Courtesy of Richard F. Moreno, of the Nevada Commission on Tourism

NEW HAMPSHIRE

"OCEAN-BORN" MARY'S HOUSE

This magnificent eighteenth century Greathouse stands in a calm, ordinary countryside that belies the unusual appearance of such a house. But this is no ordinary mansion. It owes its existence to a pirate named Don Pedro, said to have been a renegade of noble birth. Don Pedro, it is believed, fled his native England because he had backed the wrong political party, the Stuarts. Their attempt had failed to regain the throne from the Hanovers, and it was best he left while he still could.

In 1720, his pirate ship boarded an immigrant ship, called *The Wolf,* carrying would-be settlers to the new world. The people aboard were mainly Irish and Scottish, hoping for a better life overseas. John Wilson, the ship's captain, was particularly anxious to make port since his wife had recently given birth to a child which had not yet been baptized. Upon hearing this, the pirate asked Mrs. Wilson to name the baby Mary, after his beloved mother. In return, he would spare the ship, the crew, and the

Photos by Hans Holzer
The house
stones in the garden, allegedly marking where Don Pedro buried his loot.

valuables aboard. A deal was struck, much to the dismay of the less generously inclined pirate crew.

The baby grew up to be a lovely woman, and she married a man named Wallace. Years later Don Pedro, who had kept in touch with the Wilsons all through the years, came to Henniker, New Hampshire, and built himself a mansion with the help of his ship's carpenters. When Mr. Wallace left Mary a widow, she and Don Pedro lived happily in the mansion. Later a disgruntled former pirate crew member did Don Pedro in, leaving everything in Mary's hands.

Mary Wallace died in 1814, but she never quite left. The house was owned by a succession of people and the present owners prefer to remain nameless. They persistently deny there is any ghost in the house, mainly because of the unwanted attention, especially on Halloween nights.

But a number of responsible witnesses have seen "Oceanborn" Mary looking after "her" house. A state trooper saw her standing in the window looking out toward him; as he approached the house. Two visitors came to see the famous mansion which was closed at the time. Nevertheless, they were taken through the house by a tall lady in a white dress—none other than the original owner, of course.

I have been to the house several times, in the company of some very fine psychics, and the story is that Mary Wallace feels it is *still* her house. But she does not seem to mind occasional visitors.

MYSTERY HILL, THE AMERICAN STONEHENGE

D ue to the persistent efforts of Robert E. Stone of Derry, New Hampshire, the site he later came to call Mystery Hill was saved for posterity. Through the years valuable research was done to establish it as a genuine Ibero-Celtic site very much like the original Stonehenge in England.

The hill on which the elaborate maze of buildings, or their remnants, now stand, was once free of trees. There are monoliths called dolmens marking the four seasons, for the main purpose of the site was that of an observatory, just like the one in Britain. Through careful examination of inscriptions and rock drawings found here, and a test called "radiocarbon 14 dating," there is no doubt that these structures were erected sometime between 3000 and 1500 B.C.

Even though the traditional archaeological establishment wishes it would all go away, this site, along with other ancient artifacts and ruins all along the east coast, has long proved that Columbus was probably the last explorer to come to America, rather than the first.

There are subterranean chambers, priest's speakers tubes, a sacrificial table and much more to see. The Ibero-Celtic inscriptions are quite clear and the people who inscribed the stones probably came from Portugal and Spain. This was after their original homelands, Phoenicia and the island of Crete, had suffered damage from earthquakes and floods.

Mystery Hill is only about a ten-minute ride from the town of Salem, New Hampshire.

Photos by Hans Holzer and Osborn Stone

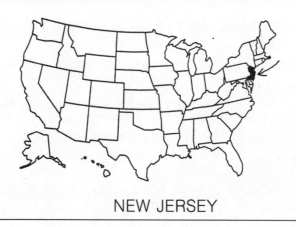

NEW JERSEY

GARRETT MOUNTAIN

Passaic County, New Jersey boasts a rather remarkable parkland area, which the Park Commission carefully oversees from its current headquarters at Lambert Castle. The castle is a nineteenth century Greathouse built during the Industrial Revolution by a wealthy businessman from England.

The park is extensive and can be entered from entrances with such colorful names as Squirrelwood Road and Weasel Drift Road.

When I first heard about the mysterious goings-on inside the park, which is relatively untouched woodland on both sides of a comfortable central road, I made arrangements to visit it in the company of a clairvoyant. The then director, Ronald F. Dooney, was most sympathetic to our quest and opened the gates for us after dark, when our party—and the ghosts—were the only ones about.

In August of 1976, two young men named Victor Tartaglia and Joe Grosso, were driving their car out of Garrett Mountain

Park toward the Weasel Drift Road exit around midnight. The park was supposed to be closed but one gate was still open and they were heading for it. They rounded a bend and saw a hunched figure that seemed to be limping. Since they did not want to hit the person, they slowed down until they got closer. Their car lights plainly showed them several things: they could see right through the man; he had an injured arm; and was wearing a colonial soldier's uniform. When the lights hit the figure, he turned toward the car, putting out his other arm as if to signal them for help. They were quite close now and realized the man's body seemed to radiate and his eyes were like "glowing eggs", as they both recalled it.

That was too much for them. They stepped on the gas and high-tailed it out of the park.

I decided to investigate their experience and discovered that a colonial military encampment had once been at the spot where they had their ghostly encounter.

On April 28, 1984, I came to the spot with my psychic friend, Kathy Koehler, who knew nothing of the story. She clairvoyantly described the area as it looked in the eighteenth century. The man, she said, was named John James Cranston. The year was 1786, and the uniform was that of the militia, not the regular army. Apparently he had been knifed by an Indian fighter and although he killed the man, Cranston did not realize he himself was also dead. At the time the two young men encountered him, he was evidently looking for help, not realizing how much time had elapsed since his traumatic experience.

Since the area was fought over numerous times during the latter part of the eighteenth century, chances are that a sensitive person could re-experience some of the events, if not actually run into a ghost or two. Mr. and Mrs. Kurt Schuster and Cynthia Lightbody, who visited the area in 1992, also "felt" the presence of pre-revolutionary occurrences.

NASSAU HALL, PRINCETON UNIVERSITY

Built in 1756 and resembling a stately mansion, or a European palace, Nassau Hall was the first building of what was to become Princeton University. It was also the largest building of its kind in the American Colonies at the time of the Revolution.

But long before it became a seat of learning and research, Princeton served as the emerging nation's capital. From June to November 1783, Princeton was the capital of the Thirteen Colonies.

During the Revolutionary War the hall sheltered troops of both sides. At the time, many saw the war as a civil war between Yankees who wanted complete independence from Britain, and Tories who wanted limited self-rule but preferred to remain loyal to the Crown.

Congress was in session here at Nassau Hall, awaiting word regarding the peace negotiations then going on in Paris, France. It was here that they received word of the signing of the Treaty of Paris which ended the Revolutionary War.

It might be that a sensitive person could feel or even re-experience the emotional atmosphere of this period when visiting the hall.

Photo by Robert F. Matthews, Courtesy of Princeton University.

THE STONEHENGE INCIDENT

The Stonehenge Apartments in suburban Edgewater, New Jersey have absolutely nothing in common with their namesake in Salisbury Plain. The tall, tower-like building dates back to the 1960s, and it is simply one of several tall apartment towers built on top of the Palisades facing Manhattan across the Hudson River. For a view of the New York City skyline, you can't beat the location.

What makes the Stonehenge Apartments a place of mystery, however, happened for the first time on January 5, 1975. Driving home after a day's work of running his liquor store nearby, George O'Barski noticed a strange aircraft overhead that seemed to hover and then suddenly disappear from the area. What he saw that late afternoon was no ordinary plane. Still, he dismissed the matter, figuring that perhaps the U.S. Air-Force was trying out something new and unusual.

Precisely a year later in January 1976, however, something more ominous took place. This time Mr. O'Barski observed the goings-on from the ground. The "contraption" was indeed there again, hovering over a small park known as the North Hudson Park situated directly in front of the Stonehenge Apartments. It is just an ordinary park, narrow and planted with trees and shrubbery like so many others. As Mr. O'Barski watched with mounting fascination, but without any apprehension or fear, he noticed a ladder being lowered from the aircraft. Suddenly "six or seven little people", who looked like children to O'Barski rushed down the ladder and into the park. There they scooped up earth and plants with some sort of shovel and rapidly returned up the ladder to their aircraft. The ladder was pulled in and then the craft took off with a very loud bang.

The "little people" wore strange overcoats and headgear,

Photo by Hans Holzer

Mr. O'Barski reported when he was interviewed later that day by a local television channel.

While this was going on in mid-morning, the doorman at the Stonehenge Apartments stood inside the large glass front entrance, as was his duty. William Palowski, the doorman, was just thinking how boring his job was, when the strange aircraft took off with a loud bang, which he clearly heard. At the same time, the huge glass front entrance shattered into thousands of pieces!

The incident was immediately investigated by a knowing reporter from the New York *Village Voice,* together with the well-known UFO authority and investigator, Budd Hopkins.

But the UFO wasn't the only thing that disappeared quite suddenly—so did the news coverage by all the other television channels. There was not a word in the rest of the press either.

Evidently someone in government wanted it that way to keep the populace from finding out about aircraft they could not control.

NEW MEXICO

INSCRIPTION ROCK AT EL MORRO

Some thirty-five miles east of the Zuni reservation rises a sandstone butte which has inscriptions from a variety of people. Perhaps its sudden strange appearance in the middle of the plains impressed the people who passed by here.

The first inscription left on the rock was a record of the journey of General Don Juan de Onate, in 1605, when he was on his way toward the Gulf of California. There are altogether some five hundred Spanish inscriptions left by travellers, some disappointed at not finding the fabled golden cities they had been told about. They found only that the "gold" was the sun's reflection on the reddish walls of ancient Indian pueblos!

Most of the travellers who engraved their names on this rock were en route further west toward California. They were from all walks of life—officers, soldiers, and tradesmen, hoping to find their own version of El Dorado somewhere over the horizon. Most of them never did, and only their names, and sometimes the dates of their passing through here, are left today.

THE "SKY CITY" OF ACOMA

Situated on top of a steep mesa, or solitary rock, there lies an ancient Indian village, dating back long before the conquistadores. Obviously, the village was built high in the sky to protect it from enemies, both native and foreign, and it was already very ancient when Coronado's troops came here around 1540. Radiocarbon 14 dating tests show it to have been there by 1000 A.D. The only way for people to get up to the top of the mesa was by a precarious path cut into the steep side of the rock, barely enough for toes and fingers to get a good hold. This is called the "ladder trail," and it is not recommended to the average visitor!

The Indians thought they were safe, but Don Juan de Onate and his men found another pathway up the mesa and killed most of the people living there—a fine Spanish colonial custom. The Acoma natives had been considered a most "rebellious" group by the conquerors.

Today, the "city in the sky," which rises four hundred feet, is empty but for the memories of past events.

Three miles northeast of Azuma, New Mexico is a second mesa of equal height called "The Enchanted Mesa." This sandstone butte is considered by the Acoma tribe to be the home of their ancestors. But a long time ago a sandstorm destroyed the access to the top of the mesa, and it is devoid of any people now.

Photo Courtesy of Mark Nohl of the New Mexico Economic and Tourism Department

THE LARGEST PRE-HISTORIC APARTMENT HOUSE IN AMERICA

The Chaco Canyon area in New Mexico was a center of thriving native communities until the twelfth century when the region was abandoned for unknown reasons.

Twelve pre-historic apartment house ruins have been found here, located sixty-four miles north of Thoreau.

This sophisticated settlement was able to accommodate large numbers of people in relatively small areas. The Pueblo Bonito, for instance, housed at least twelve hundred people in eight hundred rooms and also had 32 kivas or public rooms within its walls.

Theirs was a highly-developed, quasi-urban civilization, with each family group having its own apartment. Yet all were interconnected both spiritually and physically, the latter by intricate bridges and passages between the various buildings. In a sense, this was a commune, a closely-knit community who shared amenities as well as beliefs. Those who came later were unwilling or unable to live together peacefully in such large numbers. They found the place empty and abandoned when they arrived, and they used it as best they could. But the soul of the commune was no longer there. Those who had built the place had taken it with them.

The mystery remains—why did the population leave after building this vast and sophisticated complex? Where did they go?

Photo Courtesy of Mark Nohl of the New Mexico Economic and Tourism Department

THE LOURDES OF AMERICA

Located in a Spanish colonial town called Chimayo, near Española, there stands the church called El Sanctuario de Chimayo. It was built in this seventeenth century town by a well-to-do family in 1816. But it is not just the architecture of this rural church nor its fine art which has attracted people from all over, it is the alleged curative power of the site.

In a small room near the altar are the crutches and canes left behind by people who came here to be cured, and who walked away, cured. There is also a hole in the ground of this chamber where pilgrims take samples of the soil, considered miraculous. A well is also nearby, and it is likely that the natural radiation in the soil has curative value, for no healing sanctuary can maintain its reputation without results.

The Tewa Pueblo people who lived in this area have always considered the site to be sacred. It was a healing center long before the church was erected over it.

Photo Courtesy of Mark Nohl of the New Mexico Economic and Tourism Department

NEW YORK

THE SOLDIER BURIED ON FIFTH AVENUE

We know who is buried in Grant's Tomb, of course. Groucho Marx told us. But what about that odd-looking monument on Fifth Avenue at the corner of Twenty-fifth Street? To the casual observer it looks like a monument in honor of something or someone, but very few New Yorkers know that it is not just a memorial, but also a tomb with a real body underneath.

This twenty-foot-tall, tapered, concrete obelisk stands in the middle of Fifth Avenue, with traffic whizzing by on all sides.

The man buried underneath is William Jenkins Worth, a Mexican-American War hero who was said by his contemporaries to have looked good on horseback. They referred to him as "the Murat of the American Army." Considering that Joachim Murat, Napoleon's brother-in-law, ended up being shot by a firing squad, that nickname could not have been without drawbacks. Be this as it may, Worth did serve in the Mexican-American War, and did rather well. When he returned to New York

Photo by Hans Holzer

96

City in 1849, having come through the war without a scratch, he promptly died. So shocked was the city government by the sudden demise of their local hero, that they decided to erect a monument over his grave to honor him for posterity. However, rumor has it he was not at all well liked by his contemporaries in the city and the burial plot was not meant exactly as an honor. After all, who wants to find eternal rest in the middle of traffic?

THE "NATURAL" TELEPHONE IN GRAND CENTRAL STATION

G rand Central Station in New York City between Lexington and Vanderbilt Avenues on Forty-second Street isn't what it used to be. Not as many leave or arrive here now, but it is still a busy place even if the trains are mainly suburban. Lots of people meet each other in Grand Central because it is centrally located and easy to find.

There are two levels from which trains depart, connected by stairs and a slanting corridor. The lower level has fewer shops and restaurants than the larger, more oppulent main floor, but both levels have lots of pay telephones in corners along the walls.

While it is true you need a coin to operate the pay phones, you can talk to someone across the wide corridor without any money. Just stand in one corner, facing the wall, and speak. Your voice will travel along the vaulted roof of the supporting beams and be heard clearly by someone standing in the opposite corner!

Photo by Hans Holzer

MOVE OVER, CALIFORNIA

Whenever earthquake zones are mentioned, California is high on the list of sites. A psychosis, about California falling into the sea after an earthquake, has developed among many people living on the West Coast. The truth is, there are fault lines underneath the California soil and earthquakes do occur frequently.

One hears very rarely about earthquakes on the east coast. An occasional rumbling in Connecticut, or a little hysteria about New Madrid and its impending doom, make headlines in the press for a day or two.

Nevertheless, even rock-solid Manhattan, the heart of New York City, sits atop a fault line. It runs below Fourteenth Street up to Eighty-fifth Street on the west side. Thus far, it has lain dormant, and the last report of any kind of earth tremor goes back to the middle nineteenth century. We don't even know if it had anything to do with the fault. There can be other causes for earth tremors such as sink holes, water damage, or shifts in the soil.

The highly-respected prophet Edgar Cayce predicted an earthquake in New York City sometime toward the end of this century. Is it possible? Possible, yes. Probable, no. That is, unless man does something foolish, like building atomic energy plants on top of fault lines. The one in Long Island at Shoreham, close enough to Manhattan to be dangerous, has recently been shut down. Maybe that is what Cayce saw?

Photo by Hans Holzer
1) Eighty-fifth Street and Riverside Drive
2) Fourteenth Street and Fifth Avenue

THE CEMETARY IN WASHINGTON SQUARE

Washington Square sits at the bottom of Fifth Avenue in the heart of Greenwich Village in Manhattan. The real estate here is as expensive as any uptown, East or West. For more than a century, the square has been a park with benches and a fountain in the center. The entrance was marked by a large triumphal arch modelled after similar arches in Paris and ancient Rome.

The campus of New York University surrounds the square and park on two sides, with expensive and landmark old private houses on the other two sides. In the summer, strolling musicians, chess players and artists occupy the area, demonstrating their skills or displaying their wares. It's as close to Montmartre as New York City can come.

Picture everybody's surprise when, a few years ago, a team from New York University started to look for colonial artifacts as part of a study course. This was meant merely to enhance the attractiveness of the area by tying it in with our past.

However, they found a cemetary dating back to pre-revolutionary times, including numerous skeletons, all laid out neatly in rows. What was one to do? Restoring the area to its pre-revolutionary purpose was not likely to reassure the souls of the departed. Leaving it as it was would not do either, since tourists would not be likely to visit a graveyard.

A truly Salomonian decision was made—the site was covered up again. The skeletons stayed in place, and the living could continue to enjoy the park.

Photographs by Hans Holzer

THE STRANGE STREET SIGNS IN GREENWICH VILLAGE

There are lots of strange things in and about Greenwich Village, Manhattan, the center of the downtown creative communities.

For one thing, there are a number of ancient haunted houses in this very old section of the city, and most of these historic houses are now safe from the wreckers. The one that got away, however, was Alexander Hamilton's doctor's house where Hamilton had expired. I first visited the lovely townhouse in the late 1960s to deal with its ghost. But then came the wreckers and presto, the house vanished. Alex presumably (but not certainly) vanished also, and now an ugly little apartment house disgraces the spot, one would hope, half empty.

But the inconsistency of Village life and mores extends beyond its historic houses to some of its public street signs, seemingly without bothering anyone in authority.

The corner where Fourth Street crosses Tenth Street is just an ordinary street corner, and it so happens that Fourth Street is the stranger here, curving around Tenth Street for a block or so in defiance of ordinary street procedure. Just a few blocks away there is Waverly Place, crossing—Waverly Place, for similar reasons. Picture the poor tourist or uptown visitor (same thing) looking for a certain number on these streets. Only a native knows . . . not even The Shadow does!

Photographs by Hans Holzer

104

THE SONNENBERG MANSION

There is a magnificent, old, five-story mansion at 19 Irving Place on New York City's Gramercy Park, a private oasis of elegance and quiet. It is open only to the people living immediately adjacent to the park and they alone get keys to the gates. The house was built in the Federal style, during the first half of the nineteenth century and has retained its original distinguished appearance.

As time went on, the building changed hands, until some thirty years or so ago it quietly passed into the hands of the very colorful and justly famous theatrical publicist Ben Sonnenberg. He cherished the mansion and lavished money and effort on it so that it became known henceforth simply as "the Sonnenberg mansion."

But then Mr. Sonnenberg died. It had been his last wish to be buried on the grounds of his beloved residence. This was illegal, so the matter had to be dealt with prudently and quietly. Mr. Sonneberg's earthly remains found their final resting place underneath the bushes on the side of the building facing directly onto Gramercy Park. The exact location, that is, which bush he was under, remained forever a secret.

The building was now up for sale, the contents, alas being auctioned off separately, thus destroying the atmosphere of integrity between house and furnishings Mr. Sonnenberg had spent so many years and much money on to develop. But so it went, and now the house stood, empty, naked, as naked as some of the ladies of the stage Mr. Sonnenberg fancied, must have been at various times in the upper chambers.

The property now became the property of an Austrian baron, whose main claim to fame (aside from his bank account) had been his skill in developing commercially-viable perfumes. The baron had become the owner and main beneficiary of the Evyan Perfumes Company. It was his intention to move his headquarters into the mansion at some future date.

Meanwhile, the house was in the care of a young couple, who occupied a small flat at the rear of the building in what must have once been the servants' quarters.

The husband contacted me about some strange happenings. An attractive lady had apparently appeared on the staircase and then disappeared suddenly, at a time when nobody but he and his wife were about. There were footsteps and doors being opened and shut all the time by unseen hands.

On a quiet, chilly, evening in March 1982, I came to the mansion in the company of a psychic lady friend who might prove helpful.

I took pictures in the now-empty library and suddenly "felt" I should look for a hidden wall safe. The custodian, surprised at my request, pulled back the drapes covering the French windows, and there was the wall safe! I took a picture of the wall safe but when the picture came back from the lab, there was a naked woman's arm extended toward the safe—as if to protect it!

I assured the caretakers that the ghost lady was no threat to anyone. As for Mr. Sonnenberg, he got his wish to be buried on the premises so why would he want to haunt the place? But I decided to make my report to the owners of the building, the Evyan Perfumes Company. The owner had become ill and his staff were far from grateful for my offer of help in respect to the ghost or ghosts.

The baron passed away but Evyan Perfumes moved their headquarters into the Sonnenberg mansion anyway.

They even put their company name over the door, something Ben Sonnenberg might have readily understood. The house now seems eerily quiet, perhaps even empty. You can see for yourself what goes on at the former Sonnenberg mansion. Just don't expect much help from management. But I suspect the resident ghosts don't care much about that either.

MOTHER CABRINI'S BODY

Up near 190th Street, in the Washington Heights section of Manhattan, stands the proper, imposing edifice of the St. Frances Xavier Cabrini Chapel. This chapel is maintained by the order of the Missionary Sisters of the Sacred Heart of Jesus, the society Mother Cabrini founded many years before in her native Italy. Born in the town of Lodi, Italy, she did a great deal of work with the poor and sick, founded hospitals in several American cities and eventually became the first American saint, having become an American citizen.

Mother Cabrini died in 1917 and was canonized by the Pope in 1946. As the first female American saint, she has become the patroness of immigrants, especially those coming to America.

Mother Cabrini had been buried in Italy after her death in 1917, but in 1933 her body was transferred to America, to the school chapel at 701 Fort Washington Avenue. What was remarkable was that her body was intact fifteen years after her interment. This was considered to be a miracle. People from all over came by to pray and ask for intercessions, so much so that a larger church had to be built to accommodate both the body and the visitors who come to look at it. So it is under the main altar of the present, larger church that her body now rests.

That is, however, not all of it. Her head and hands are in Rome, Italy, since that is where the Order has its headquarters. In the New York location, head and hands are waxen replicas, but the rest of the body is the real thing.

One can only marvel at the dexterity of the religiously oriented mind to accept such accommodations. But then most of good old St. Nick lies in Bari, Italy, except for a couple bones left behind by grave robbers when they left Turkey in a hurry with

Photographs Courtesy of St. Frances Xavier Cabrini Chapel

most of the bones, which to this day are still buried in Demre, Turkey.

It is said that a visit to the shrine of Mother Cabrini is not only a religiously-uplifting experience for the faithful, but may well result in the healing of body and soul.

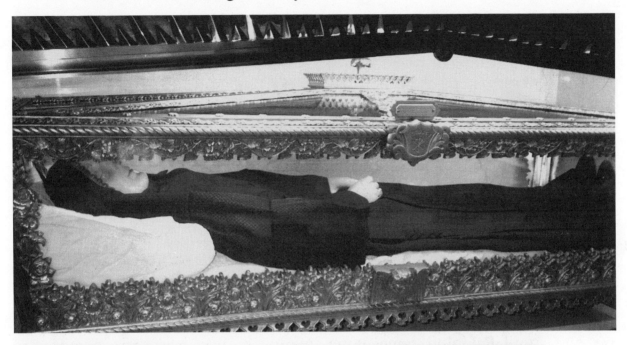

THE BIRTHPLACE OF SANTA'S REINDEER

In 1822, Dr. Clement C. Moore, returning from medical visits to his lovely old home in Elmhurst, Queens, just over the East River from Manhattan, felt a muse coming on.

So he sat down at his desk and started to compose a lovely poem, which we know today as "A Visit from St. Nicholas." It was meant for his own children, but a friend saw it and before long the poem was published in *The Troy Sentinel,* a newspaper, and it was an immediate success. Christmas simply would not be the same without it.

The mode of Santa Claus's transportation, and his reindeer, including their names, were the invention of Dr. Moore, and not until Rudolph came along in our century, was there a more popular group of Christmas animals.

When I was a teenager in Elmhurst, Moore's old wooden barn was still standing although the house itself was long gone. Today, the barn is gone too, replaced by a subway stop.

If you visit the spot which has been turned into a small park, say a prayer for Dr. Moore, and for his imaginary reindeer.

Photo Courtesy of the Queens Historical Society

THE OLD MERCHANT'S DAUGHTER

If you happen to be in the vicinity of the Bowery in New York City, preferably in daytime, drop in the Old Merchant's House located at 29 East Fourth Street. This magnificent house, once owned by Samuel Tredwell, is now a museum. In its heyday, it was a standout residence and became known for the fact that its owner had no use for gentlemen suitors interested in his daughters—Sarah, Gitty (really Gertrude), and Phoebe.

Gertrude outlived the rest of the family and lived alone in the house to a ripe old age. But long after her death, people visiting the house reported seeing a woman of her description looking at them. She was seen staring out from the magnificent Duncan Phyfe staircase, and standing in the area where her own clothes are carefully preserved under glass.

I have been to the house several times with different mediums, and the story is pretty much the same. It was dramatized by Henry James in his novel *Washington Square,* made immortal by a film in which Olivia de Havilland played the ghostly Gertrude.

Shut for a while for renovations, the house is again open to visitors under the stewartship of Margaret Halsey Gardiner, the executive director, mainly Sunday afternoons or by appointment. But you don't need an appointment with the ghost.

Photo by Hans Holzer

THE CONFERENCE HOUSE ON STATEN ISLAND

Picture this—the Revolutionary War is about to break out. The British are in New York, and the Yankees or patriots are in New Jersey. Staten Island, in between, is still no-man's land. The date is September 11, 1776.

Lord Richard Howe, the commander of the British fleet, wants to find a solution to the conflict. He gets permission to meet with the opposite side for one last attempt to settle their differences. The rebel side consists of Benjamin Franklin, who is also for peace, the temperamental John Adams, and Edward Rutledge.

They met at a house, built in the 1670s for Captain Christopher Billopp, a Dutchman in English service. His descendants eventually lost the house since they sided with the Crown against the patriots, and we all know who won the war.

Originally called Bentley Manor, the Conference House is located in what is now Tottenville. I have been to this remarkable house several times with different psychics to check out the reported incidents of hauntings. These include a servant girl allegedly killed in a sudden rage by Captain Billopp, some Indians whose skeletons were found nearby, and someone who likes to rearrange the table silver downstairs when nobody is around. I am not sure of his identity, though he must know something about the house and its contents.

The Conference House can be visited by the public on most afternoons, but one must call the Conference House Association first (718-984-2086).

Photos Courtesy of The Conference House Association

THE MARTYRS' SHRINE

Although Mother Cabrini was the first American woman saint, there were earlier canonizations of male Americans, and the site at the village of Auriesville, just north of Albany, honors their deaths at the hands of the hostile Mohawk Indians.

Believing that the site of such an event creates an atmosphere of religious power, the shrine has become a popular pilgrimage site recognized even by the present Pope.

It all began in August 1642 when two Jesuit missionaries from Canada were captured by the Mohawks and brought to what was then called the village of Ossernenon. They were Father Isaac Jogues and Father Rene Goupil, both of French birth. They, along with another priest, John LaLande, were killed by the Mohawks.

What got the Jesuits into trouble in the first place was their insistence on converting the native Americans to the Catholic faith. Had they left the Indians alone to their ancient spiritual ways, the three Jesuits, along with five others from Canada, might have lived to a ripe old age.

On the spot of their death a martyrs' shrine was begun in 1885. In 1931 a huge church, able to accommodate 6,500 worshippers, was erected.

The altar of this church, the Coliseum, is built to resemble the palisades which used to surround the Mohawk villages for protection.

As if to make up for the slaughter of the Jesuits, the site is also renowned for the birth in 1656 of an Indian saint, Kateri Tekakwitha. He was the son of a Christian Algonquin mother and a Mohawk chief.

Photos Courtesy of the Auriesville Martyrs' Shrine

THE ANGRY INDIAN CHIEF OF AMITYVILLE

A Dutch Colonial house was built at 112 Ocean Avenue in the town of Amityville, Long Island. The land is an old native American cemetary, but the developers didn't care. The people living there never find peace in it—there are suicides, divorces, and people moving in and out. A powerful Indian chief was buried on his horse, upright, with all the honors due him. Time passes, there is a heavy rainfall, and the skeleton's head peaks out from the soil. Along comes a youngster who breaks it off and plays football with it, not realizing what he has done. This is one explanation for the problems. If you're that Indian chief, now supposedly residing in the Happy Hunting Ground, you wouldn't like it and you'd probably raise hell.

Then the house is moved elsewhere in town and all becomes serene. On the lot, however, another house is built in 1928, roughly thirty years after the Indian chief lost his head. Eventually, the DeFeo family moves in, but never finds much peace in it. The father brings in a priest and plants lilies in the garden, but the priest is driven out by unknown forces and the flowers die overnight.

On November 13, 1974, the eighteen-year-old son Ronald gets up in the middle of the night, takes a rifle, and methodically shoots every one of the six members of his family. As he moves from room to room, nobody tries to run, nobody tries to escape, and nobody in the neighborhood hears any shots.

Eventually, Ronald was convicted of the mass murders, although he claims not to remember doing it. The case has all the earmarks of possession—an emotionally unstable young man, a family full of internal dissent, and a vengeful Indian chief bent on destroying anyone daring to live on his land. Building houses on Indian cemeteries is always risky business. I was the first to bring a reputable trance medium, the late Ethel Johnson Myers, to the

Photos by Hans Holzer

house on January 15, 1977, at the request of the defense attorneys for young DeFeo. DeFeo had gotten 25 years to life and the attorneys hoped I might help reopen the case on the grounds that Ronald DeFeo, while guilty of murder, was under the influence of the Indian spirit. But it never happened, though I did see DeFeo in prison and am convinced he was indeed in a state of involuntary trance when he committed the crimes.

After getting all that publicity in the media, not to mention the books, and three movies—two of them based on my stories—two things occurred: the people in the house who had bought it cheaply and did not believe in anything supernatural, were being bothered by masses of curious tourists and resented it. They finally altered the street number on the house, but to no avail. The other "problem" was an influx of self-styled investigators, ranging from a salesman from Elmhurst with a phony doctorate, who called himself a Vampyrist, to a team from Connecticut. This team consisted of a former artist turned "demonologist", accompanied by his psychic wife and a priest dismissed from his diocese, and occasionally an off-duty police officer. Their "expertise" was just one more nuisance to the people in the house. The house is now empty again . . . except, of course, for the enraged Indian chief who is still looking for his skull. Amityville can be reached by car, bus and train, and Ocean Avenue is easy to find. But don't say I sent you.

THE MYSTERIOUS BAT AT THE POUGHKEEPSIE RECTORY

In Poughkeepsie, a two-hour drive north of New York City, there is an Episcopal church called Christ Church. It has an adjacent rectory, all built of solid redstone found in the quarries of the area.

In 1947, the long-time rector of the church died of old age, and the position was filled by Bishop James Pike. Pike spent two-and-half years there, but not without some very curious incidents.

It seems that the previous rector was a very austere, Protestant clergyman, whereas Jim Pike, a former Roman Catholic, liked the romantic, theatrical aspects of the service. Immediately on taking over, Pike changed things around, putting flower wreaths and candles on the main altar—something his predecessor would never have tolerated.

Sure enough, the old man was dead, but not gone, apparently. The candles kept being blown out by an unseen force even though there was no wind or open windows in the church. None of this particularly bothered Pike, who had not yet dealt with the psychic world to any extent. When he persisted with his changes in the church, the resistance took a decidedly unusual turn.

Finding himself alone in the library of the church one evening, Jim Pike suddenly noticed that he had the company of a good-sized bat flying about madly in the library, as if to annoy him. Immediately Pike checked the windows and found them closed. There was only one door to the library, and he had closed it when he had entered. So where did the animal come from?

Clearly, the bat wanted him out of the library, and it eventually succeeded in chasing Pike out. He shut the door behind him, still hearing the mad flappings. When he cautiously returned an hour or so later, and opened the only door to the library, the bat

Photos by Hans Holzer

was gone—but how? Try as he would, Pike and his staff found no opening, no crevice, no way the bat could have entered or left the library.

I came to know the Bishop well and he assured me that the bat could have been none other than his predecessor. At the very least, he could have been sent by him, to annoy Jim because of his activities in changing things around in the rectory and church.

I later visited the rectory in the company of the late medium Ethel Johnson Myers. Through her, the very angry spirit of Pike's predecessor complained bitterly about the changes in "his" church.

RAYNHAM HALL

In the lovely Long Island town of Oyster Bay stands a restored saltbox house built in 1738 by the Townsend family. They were prominent members of British aristocracy and had now extended their domain to the colonies.

Five generations of Townsends lived there, but eventually the house passed into the hands of the town of Oyster Bay, which maintains it as a museum. It is an authentic house of the period and worth visiting on its own merits.

However, there is a persistent story of a love affair between a Townsend girl named Sally and John Simcoe, a British officer in league with British master spy John Andre, who did indeed visit the house. Certain disturbances of a ghostly nature have been reported, which is not so unusual for an old house where much history has transpired. But Andre did not die there, and the suggestion that it is his ghost somehow come back to haunt Raynham Hall is preposterous.

The reported disturbances may well have another explanation. There is another, more magnificent Raynham Hall, still standing in all its glory in Yorkshire, England. This is the property of the Marquess of Townsend family, and it is still haunted by the unhappy spirit of Dorothy Walpole, sister of the famous Prime Minister. She had been shut up in a room upstairs to die in madness.

Perhaps the most famous authenticated ghost photograph was taken at the English Raynham Hall by two photographers hired to take random pictures of the mansion. In the photograph we can plainly see the white figure of a woman descending the staircase, transparent, but looking very much as Lady Walpole looked in life.

The picture has been published many times all over the world, including a 1936 issue of *Life* magazine.

Photo Courtesy of the Friends of Raynham Hall

It is true that ghosts don't travel but the ghost of Dorothy Walpole has not been reported in Yorkshire for many years. Could it be that somehow she has managed to impress her presence in that sister house, also called Raynham Hall, in Oyster Bay?

Frankly, I doubt it, but then some member of the Townsend family from the old country might have drawn her in when coming to the new world.

One thing is certain—wherever the spirit of Major John Andre dwells now, it is not likely to be Raynham Hall in Oyster Bay. After all, he was *just visiting*.

THE SACRED GROVE OF THE MORMONS

Palmyra was an ancient Greek city in Asia Minor known for both its remoteness and the fact that a strange government existed there during the third century A.D., and even before. It was around 270 that Palmyra's Queen Zenobia held forth with powers far beyond the geographic importance of her "kingdom." Even the powerful Roman Emperor Aurelian respected her and made her his ally.

Palmyra, New York would not be of much importance, were it not for the fact that it contains some of the most important holy sites of the Mormon religion.

Joseph Smith lived in this town with his parents, who were simple country folk. But Joseph was curious about a lot of things, and as sometimes happens, his rich imagination and curiosity were far greater than his little hometown could normally satisfy. When he was fourteen years old, while investigating the various churches of his time, Joseph claimed to have had a spiritual vision in which God and Jesus appeared to him and in effect told him that none of the existing churches were any good. Seven years later, in 1827, he had another encounter, Smith reported, in which an angel by the name of Moroni appeared to him and told him that ancient records, inscribed on golden tablets, were buried nearby under a stone on a hill named Cumorah. Moroni said that Joseph would in good time be told to retrieve them and translate them for all to know.

Of course, he did, although the tablets were seen by him alone and later taken back by the angel Moroni. They allegedly contained characters in ancient Egyptian, Chaldaic, and Arabic, all at the same time, which would be a tremendous shock to trained archaeologists. But the tablets were never seen except by Smith so we will never know. From these characters, Smith translated and wrote the Book of Mormon, named after the father of

Photos Courtesy of the Hill Cumorah Visitors Center and Historical Sites
The Sacred Grove

this angel, Moroni. He founded, with others, the Church of the Latter-Day Saints, or Mormon Church.

While the matter of the ancient tablets purporting to tell the history of a people living here prior to 420 A.D. is a matter of faith rather than scientific evidence, the nature of the visions or apparitions reported by Joseph Smith matches such experiences described by others.

I am indebted to Mormon Church Elder L. M. Udell for the information that from this unusual and humble beginning the Mormon Church now has over eight million members, and is the third largest Christian church in the United States. Palmyra has many interesting sites to attract visitors and students of the Mormon claims.

If God did indeed chose this little New York town to create a companion religion to orthodox Christianity, he picked a most peaceful and even romantic spot to do so. Perhaps the town was part of Joseph Smith's inspiration to be a writer, to be someone with a message and to reach out to people in ways the older, unimaginative and dogmatic faiths had not.

The Hill Cumorah in Palmyra may offer psychic impressions of its past, if only of young Joseph Smith looking for those tablets.

WASHINGTON IRVING'S "SUNNYSIDE"

Washington Irving was a lawyer by training and a writer by preference. He served honorably in the War of 1812, where he befriended a fellow officer named Ichabod Crane. He thought the name was so funny he borrowed it for his fictional character who ran from the headless horseman of Sleepy Hollow.

Irving turned down a number of government offers but did eventually serve as ambassador to Spain for four years. He is the writer who invented Father Knickerbocker in 1809 and, while serving as a diplomat in London, wrote the story of Rip Van Winkle. In 1835, he returned to his beloved Hudson Valley, bought an old Dutch farmhouse, and spruced it up with romantic gables and decorations to make it look more like a mystic retreat. He called it his "snuggery" and dearly loved living in it. Irving died in 1859 and is buried in nearby Sleepy Hollow cemetary.

What makes Sunnyside particularly interesting to me is reports of psychic phenomena in the house that have come from several observers, especially volunteer custodians serving there. Eventually I visited with a competent psychic, and even filmed a segment of the NBC series "In Search of . . ." there. It would appear that Washington Irving, purveyor of fictional ghost stories, is so enamored of his Sunnyside home that he does not feel like leaving it at all.

Today Sunnyside is maintained by Historic Hudson Valley, a nonprofit association, and can be visited. It is about 45 minutes north of New York City.

Photos Courtesy of the Historic Hudson Valley

NORTH CAROLINA

OCRACOKE INLET

Cape Hatteras, that treacherous stretch of Carolina coast, was better known in olden times as "the graveyard of the Atlantic" because so many sailing ships were wrecked against it. Perhaps because of its dangerous reputation, which made pursuit by the forces of law somewhat more difficult, the area was also a haven for pirates, who found it exactly to their liking. In the early 1700s, pirates freely swaggered around Charles Town, terrorizing law-abiding citizens and getting away, quite literally, with murder.

The most notorious of these criminals was Edward Teach, a native of Bristol, England, better known to history as Blackbeard the Pirate. So brazen was the man that in May 1718 he and fellow buccaneer Stede Bonnet blockaded Charles Town harbor, captured five vessels, and made everyone coming or going pay for the privilege. He could do all this without worrying about the authorities, since Governor Charles Eden was his dear friend. But in the end the local citizenry, and especially the merchants, got together

Photo by Clay Nolan, Courtesy of the North Carolina Travel and Tourism Division

and persuaded the governor of Virginia, Alexander Spotswood, to help them get rid of Blackbeard. Blackbeard was shot to death after a fierce fight. Lt. Robert Maynard, the commander of the raid, then cut off Blackbeard's head and took it back home to Virginia as a trophy.

Teach's hole, the place on Ocracoke Inlet where Blackbeard lived when he wasn't out pirating, is worth a visit. If you see a headless pirate there, pay him no heed—he's only a ghost looking for the rest of him.

THE "LOST COLONY" OF ROANOKE ISLAND

Few historical events have been shrouded in as much mystery as the fate of the very first settlers on Roanoke Island.

Today, a play called *The Lost Colony*, re-enacts the events of that long-ago period and draws thousands of tourists to the area. But the real story is the mystery of what became of the original people.

In the 1580s, England was often bested by Spain in establishing new colonies overseas, and a clamor arose in England to do something about it.

In 1583, Humphrey Gilbert, a half-brother to Sir Walter Raleigh, advocated colonizing North America. Queen Elizabeth I was more interested in having a base of operation against the Spanish, than in establishing English settlements overseas, but she allowed Raleigh to put together an expedition in 1584. This expedition landed on the island near Kitty Hawk where they found the natives friendly. The place was a kind of paradise filled with vegetation and fowl, not to mention wild grapes which could be turned into wine. This first contact was soon followed by further landings.

Eventually, the new arrivals and the local Indians were no longer so friendly. A fort was built. Fifteen soldiers were left behind when things became too difficult for many, and the English ships returned home. In 1586 Raleigh managed to pull together another expedition. When the three ships, carrying 120 people, arrived, the fifteen men left behind were gone. They found one skeleton next to the demolished fort. Just the same, they decided to stay, and they cleared land and built themselves homes. The first child born in the New World was named Virginia Dare.

This was the first permanent settlement of the English in

Photo Courtesy of the North Carolina Travel Division

North America, but it turned out to be not so permanent, after all.

In 1590, after a war with Spain which resulted in the destruction of the Spanish Armada, more English came to Roanoke to see how the colonists were doing. Again, there were none left. Nobody knows what happened to them. The most plausible theory is that they left and moved north and disappeared into the native population, intermarrying with them.

No European settler touched ground here again until 1655, when colonists from Virginia moved in. As for the "lost colony," it remains lost.

THE LOST HEAD

There is a charming, rustic railroad crossing twelve miles west of the city of Wilmington that has attracted thousands of visitors, and these tourists are not necessarily railroad buffs. The railroad in question is the old Atlantic Coast Line, and the little village it runs through is called Maco.

Ever since 1867, this spot has been the scene of some strange phenomena, witnessed by hundreds of people. At night, sometimes there is a flickering light "walking" on the tracks at roughly the height where a man would carry a lantern. Someone has actually seen a hand holding such a lantern. And sometimes an approaching train can be heard, where no train was running.

Known soon enough as "The Maco Light," it attracted not only visitors and the curious, but also scientists who declared it to be nothing but swamp gas. However, this was difficult to reconcile with the reported sight of an old railroad lantern with a light burning inside, and also the fact there wasn't a swamp in the vicinity.

The popular story, based on pretty solid evidence I must add, is that the strange phenomena were the result of an incident that took place in 1867 on that very spot, the crossing, not far from a wooden railroad trestle of questionable safety spanning a nearby gulch. At that time, the railroad was still known as the Wilmington, Manchester and Augusta Railroad. The conductor of a certain train was riding the last coach—the caboose—when all of a sudden the car got separated from the train, and slowed down its movement, while the rest of the freight train sped away.

The conductor's name was Joe Baldwin, and he realized that this was a very dangerous situation. A major passenger train was due behind him on the same, single track very shortly. There was no time to lose, so Joe Baldwin grabbed the lantern and ran back on the track toward the oncoming passenger train, swinging his lantern wildly, in the hope that the engineer of the passenger train

Photo by Hans Holzer
Drawing by Catherine Buxhoeveden

would see the signal and slow down or stop.

Unfortunately, the engineer did not see the light and crashed his train into the stalled caboose. To the very last second, Joe tried to prevent the accident, totally oblivious of his own safety. He was hit by the oncoming train, and decapitated! The only victim of the crash was Joe—none of the passengers were seriously hurt. The lantern was later found a distance from the track where the impact had propelled it. Baldwin was buried in the Roman Catholic cemetary near where the track runs. That is, most of Joe got buried there. His head was never recovered.

So much for the events of 1867.

People in the area believe that the light seen above the tracks is Joe Baldwin, or rather his spirit, still trying to warn the oncoming train of the dangers ahead. Some say he is also looking for his lost head. Maybe he is doing both.

I was invited by the city of Wilmington to undertake a major investigation, back in 1964. I interviewed close to a hundred witnesses, I visited the track, I sat in a car several nights in a row, and sure enough, we saw that flickering light! I found Joe Baldwin's name in the records of the period, and I am firmly convinced that the phenomena are real.

You may want to see for yourself.

OHIO

ZOAR VILLAGE

In the early part of the nineteenth century, the turmoil in central Europe, notably the repressive regimes of most pre-1848 governments, caused the emigration of freedom-minded people to the New World. They were not so much in search of economic wealth but on a quest for a different way of life, free from religious and political tyranny.

One of these German-speaking movements was the separatist community established in Zoar Village in 1817 by Joseph Baumeler, who later anglicized his name to Bimeler. Only members of the Zoar Society could settle in this Ohio community. The people who came here were all from Württemberg in Southern Germany. They had broken with the Lutheran Church and sought a more mystical, direct relationship with God, without all the worldly and intellectual trappings. When they first arrived in Philadelphia, all three hundred of them, the local Quakers helped them along.

The Ohio village was essentially a commune, with all property belonging to the organization. The name Zoar is taken from

Photographs Courtesy of the Ohio Historical Society

the Biblical name for Lot's town of refuge, meaning "sanctuary from evil." In 1898, the society was dissolved since its descendants had found opportunities elsewhere in a wider world.

The village can be visited and it is being preserved by the Ohio Historical Society. It is located on Highway 212, halfway between Canton and Zanesville.

THE LARGEST SERPENT IN THE WORLD

This is not about the Amazon or some enterprising zoo. The largest serpent known is actually an effigy of a serpent, so large it can best be seen from the air to appreciate its size.

The Great Serpent Mound is a winding snake image almost a quarter of a mile long. It appears as an uncoiling snake holding an egg in its jaws.

This remarkable monument is located in Hillsboro, Ohio and is the work of a prehistoric people who had a thriving civilization here as early as the time of Christ. Later, the Hopewell Indians lived here and built fortifications as well as sacred burial mounds.

It is generally believed that the large serpent mound is the tomb of important leaders, priests, and medicine men, just as the pyramids were used to bury the pharaohs in Egypt.

Nothing like this exists anywhere else in the United States.

Hillsboro is due east of both Cincinnati and Dayton, and has a population of about 6000 people, not counting Indian spirits.

Photos Courtesy of the Ohio Division of Travel and Tourism

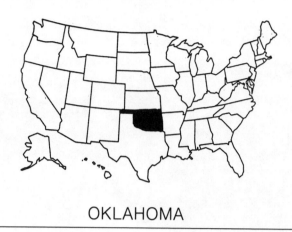

OKLAHOMA

THE DINOSAUR BURIAL GROUND

Kenton, Oklahoma is the site of a dinosaur burial ground. Located in a quarry, it contains the skeletons of these long-extinct creatures who inhabited the area ten million years ago.

Among other remains, skeletons of the seventy-foot tall Brontosaurus were discovered here. While the site retains its mysterious feeling of a past generally known to people only from books or Hollywood movies, most of the actual skeletons have been removed to the University of Oklahoma at Norman.

Kenton is near the New Mexico border in the far western part of Oklahoma near Boise City.

Photo Courtesy of Fred M. Marvel of the Oklahoma Tourism and Recreation Department

138

THE SPIRO ARTIFACTS

Practically right on the Arkansas state line, near Fort Smith, stands Spiro Rock, a remarkable collection of Indian burial mounds. There are many such mounds all over the United States, but this one is remarkably different in certain respects.

The artifacts discovered here bear a strong resemblance to Aztec artifacts found in Mexico and Guatemala. They date back to an early native-American civilization of which little is known, but they are far more sophisticated than later Indian relics. They may have been around since 1000 A.D.

The problem is that these objects do not "fit" into the area where they were discovered. Archaeologists have yet to explain why a number of artifacts, found in authentic, undisturbed locations, seem to belong to cultures and civilizations not known to have lived in these places. But the fact remains that the Spiro Artifacts are very much like those found in abundance in Central America, very far indeed from Oklahoma. It suggests that prior to the "Indians" who populated Oklahoma, there were people from Central America, or their relatives, in these same areas, who had somehow disappeared, leaving these strange artifacts as testimony to their one-time presence here.

Photographs Courtesy of Fred M. Marvel of the Oklahoma Tourism and Recreation Department

THE CAPITOL OF THE CHEROKEES

One of the great tragedies forced upon the Cherokee nation was their resettlement to the West after they had lived in Georgia for so many centuries. But the Cherokee were a strong tribe and tried to adapt to the ever-changing political landscape in the developing United States.

So when they were settled in Oklahoma, they established their nation's capital at Tahlequah.

The Cherokee had been forced out of their ancestral homelands in Georgia for purely selfish reasons by the whites: they wanted their land. So the proud Cherokee come to Oklahoma, still hurt by their forced migration. And yet, they decided to settle down and be a nation again, even in new surroundings. Their capitol building, while truly theirs, nevertheless conforms to the whites' idea of what a capitol ought to look like. It is probably one of the earliest such moves by a proud Indian nation: showing their former oppressors that they are still a nation.

Tahlequah County is due north of Muskogee, in the easternmost part of the state. What is now the Tahlequah County Courthouse was, in 1869, the capitol of the Cherokee nation.

Photograph Courtesy Fred M. Marvel, Oklahoma Tourism and Recreation Department

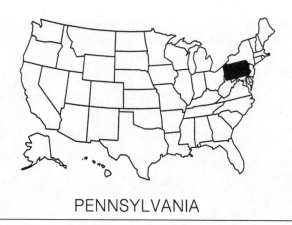

PENNSYLVANIA

THE WATERS OF BEDFORD SPRINGS

Halfway between Pittsburgh and Harrisburg, lies the small town of Bedford. In 1757 a fort was built there but it no longer exists. However, Bedford Springs was a renowned medicinal source even before the arrival of the white man. As for the little fort, like many of its kind, it was meant to protect the white settlers from "unruly" Indians.

Taking the waters at Bedford Springs was popular with Washington Society in the last century. It was supposed to "cleanse the system" from impurities. Indian tradition described it as a kind of fountain of youth—and who could resist such a claim? There was a magnificent five-story hotel which was the center of the watering place. It is hardly known today among those seeking cures for various ailments, real and imaginary. But in the nineteenth century and prior to World War I, this was indeed a place to go for whatever ailed you.

But don't ask your physician if you should take the waters at Bedford Springs—he probably never heard of it.

Photos Courtesy of The Bedford Gazette

THE OTHER GETTYSBURG

In Gettysburg, one can tour the battlefield, the historical spots, and everything is neatly laid out for you on a map. More than 2,000 markers tell you exactly where you are, what happened there, and who got killed by whom. It is possible to virtually re-live the Civil War.

But the guidebooks and booklets don't tell you that people who have visited a spot known as Little Round Top, which was where one of the bloodiest phases of the battle took place, have on occasion seen a phantom soldier still looking for his regiment, not realizing he had been killed.

And not far from the highway which leads to Harrisburg is a rustic inn called the Graeffenburg Inn. Officially, it is located in Fayetteville, on Lincoln Highway. It was named by its early owners after a spa in Austria, and there are nearby medicinal springs to warrant this designation. The inn has been in this spot for more than 150 years and has a charming, mainly Victorian interior, though its earlier construction is still evident.

A student by the name of Helen Forrest brought it to my attention some years ago. She happened to have been born in the inn, then already run as a small hotel. Helen recalls that at age five, she and her mother both heard a woman singing in her room, though no woman was visible to them. Helen's father was the manager of the inn and during his twenty-one years there he refused to rent room number 32, which had been hers as a child. During that time, a presence would open windows, move chairs, sing and leave a definite lilac scent in the air. On several occasions, Helen felt herself touched by unseen hands.

After Helen's father died, she left the inn with her mother. Subsequent managers could never make the inn pay off and two of them were smothered to death in Room 32!

Years later, Helen was doing summer stock nearby and decided to stay at the Graeffenburg Inn, where she requested and

Photos Courtesy of the National Park Service (Gettysburg) Photo by Hans Holzer (The Inn)

received her old room, number 32. That very night, she woke to someone shaking her violently. She saw no one and in panic ran out into the corridor. She turned just in time to see the drapes catch fire and the bed she had just left burst into smoke and flames. At this moment, Helen saw in the room a small woman in a "granny gown" with her hair tied back, look at her. Then the flames took over.

The room was gutted, but has since been restored. The verdict? An electrical failure. . . . In parapsychology, we call it spontaneous combustion from an intense emotional presence.

NEW GALENA ROAD

What I am about to record here is one of several examples of "time warp" experiences, where people, accidentally, wind up experiencing events in the past, not as visions, not as dreams, not as impressions or psychically.

These are substantiated cases of physical contacts with people, places, and events in what I can best describe as "the living past" although it defies all normal scientific explanation. These are not hallucinations. They are three-dimensional experiences in the present, and seem to indicate that we have still a lot to discover about the nature of time and space, Einstein notwithstanding.

New Galena Road is located in Bucks County, between Philadelphia and Doylestown. On May 11, 1967, I was contacted by Susan Hardwick of Philadelphia who wanted to share an amazing experience with me in the hope of getting some explanation. She writes:

"In the summer of 1960 I took a ride with a friend, Sal Sassani, along my favorite route. This was Route 152, starting in Philadelphia as Limekiln Pike, a beautiful, winding country road which goes way up into the mountains. I have travelled it for years and knew every curve with eyes closed! About an hour after darkness fell, I sat up stiff with a start. I knew we had not made an improper turn, yet the road was unfamiliar to me all of a sudden.

The trees were not the same. I became frightened and asked Sal to make a U-turn. As we did so, we both smelled what to us was like a combination of ether and alcohol. At the same time, the car radio fell silent! Suddenly we saw a German shepherd puppy running alongside the car. His mouth was moving but no sound was heard! Then, from our right, where there was no real road, came a ghostly shadow of a long, hearse-like car. It crossed directly in front of us and disappeared. The odor vanished and the radio came back on at the same time."

Photos Courtesy of the Bucks County Department of Parks and Recreation and William Mitchell

I responded with questions and on May 23 she contacted me again. To my question of whether she had ever had any other strange experience *at that location,* Susan Hardwick went on to report an earlier incident, which had apparently not been as frightening to her as the one later on.

"In the summer of 1958 I was driving with a friend, Jerry, on this same road, Route 152, and we turned off it into New Galena Road. Halfway toward Route 611, which is parallel to 152, we came upon a wooden building I had never seen there before. We stopped and entered and sat at a table, and my friend Jerry noticed a man who resembled his late father. We each had a Coke. This man addressed us both by our names, calling Jerry 'son,' and told him things only Jerry's father would have known. Jerry became convinced it was his father. We left and drove on a road I had never seen before, yet I knew exactly what lay around every bend and curve! The incident took place about an hour from the city. I know exactly where this spot is but I have yet to see this structure or these roads again."

I decided to come to Philadelphia with famed medium Sybil Leek and investigate the case.

On July 24, 1967, Sybil and I met up with Susan Hardwick, and a friend of hers, Barbara Heckner. I had told Sybil nothing about the case but as we were driving toward the area, I asked her if she received any kind of psychic impressions regarding it.

"This is not a ghostly phenomenon," she began, "this is a space phenomenon. . . . We're going to cross a river."

We were approaching Lancaster, Pennsylvania and no river was in sight. Five minutes later, there was the river. Sybil conveyed the feeling of masses of people in an open place, gathered for some reason, and she compared her feelings to an earlier visit to Runnymede, England, where people had gathered to sign the Magna Charta.

Now we had reached the point, forty miles from Philadelphia, where Susan had been twice before and experienced the inexplicable. What did Sybil feel about the location?

"It's a happening. . . . not a ghost . . . in the past . . . two hundred years ago . . . *out of context with time* . . . I feel detached . . . like, no man's land . . . we shouldn't be here . . . as if we were aliens in this country . . . I have to think what day it is, why we are here . . . it feels like falling off a cliff . . . I feel a large number of people in a large open space."

We began walking up an incline and Sybil indicated the vibrations from the past were stronger there.

"We are in their midst now, but these people are confused, too."

"Why are they here?"

"Unity . . . that is the word I get, Unity."

I then turned to Susan Hardwick, and asked her to point out exactly where her two experiences had taken place. This was the first time Sybil Leek heard about them in detail.

"When I drove up here in 1958 with my friend, this road we're on was not there, the road across from us was, and there was a building here, a wooden frame building that had never been there before. We felt compelled to enter somehow, and it seemed like a bar. We sat down and ordered Cokes. There were several men in the place, and my friend looked up and said, 'That man over there looks like my father.' The man then spoke to us and called us by our first names as if he knew us. He began predicting things about my friend's future and called him 'son'."

"But didn't you think there was something peculiar about all this?"

"Yes, of course we did, because Jerry's father had died when he was a baby."

"Did everything look solid to you?"

"Yes, very much so."

"How were the people dressed?"

"Country people . . . work shirts and pants."

"Were the Cokes you ordered . . . real?"

"Yes, real, modern Cokes."

I looked around. There was nothing whatever in the area remotely that looked like a wooden building.

"You're sure this is the spot, Susan?"

"Definitely, we used to picnic across the road . . . that little bridge over there is a good landmark."

"What happened then?"

"We finished our Cokes, walked out of the place, got into the car and Jerry turned to me and said, 'That was my father.' He accepted this without any criticism. So we drove off and came upon a road that I had never seen before, and have yet to see again! I have tried, but never found that road again. Then I told Jerry to stop the car and told him there would be a dilapidated farm building on the left, around the bend in the road. We proceeded to drive around it and sure enough, there it was. Then I stated there would be a lake on the right-hand side . . . and there was, too."

"Did you ever find these places again?"

"Never. I am very familiar with the area. . . . Throughout my childhood I used to come here with friends many times."

"When you left the area, was there anything unusual in the atmosphere?"

"It felt rather humid . . . but it was an August afternoon."

"Did you go back later to try and find the place again?"

"Yes. We retraced our steps, but the building was gone. The road was still there, but no building."

"Was there anything in the atmosphere that was unusual when you wandered into that wooden bar?"

"Humidity . . . an electrifying feeling. Very cool inside."

"The people?"

"The man who seemed to be Jerry's father, the bartender

and several other men sitting at the bar."

"Any writing?"

"Just signs like 'sandwiches' and different beer signs."

I thought about this for a while. Was it all an hallucination? A dream? A psychic impression? Susan assured me it was not. Both she and Jerry had experienced the same things, neither had been asleep.

"What about the people you met inside this place? How did they look to you?"

"Solid. They walked . . . and . . . that was the funny thing . . . they all stared at us as if to say, 'who are you and what are you doing here?' "

"When you first drove up here and noticed that the area was unusual, did you notice any change from the normal road to this spot?"

"Only where the stop sign is now. That did not exist. Instead there was gravel and that wooden building. It started right in from the road, maybe fifty feet from the road. Further back it was as normal as it is today. Suddenly it was there, and the next moment we were in it."

I decided to go on to the second location, not far away, where Susan's other "time warp" experience had taken place in the summer of 1960. Again, as we approached it, I asked Sybil for any impressions she might have about the area and incident.

Even though this was a different location, though still not too far from the other place, Sybil felt that "the strength of the force is constant" between the two places. But she did not feel any of the odd excitement she had earlier picked up about the first location.

Once again, Susan pointed out the clump of trees she remembered from the incident. "We were riding on this road," Susan explained, "a road by the way I have known for many years first hand. It must have been around midnight, in the middle of July, in 1960. All of a sudden, this stretch of the road *became extremely unfamiliar*. The trees were not the same anymore, they looked different, much older than they are now. There were no houses here, just completely open on the right side of the road."

There are small houses in the area she points to.

"This clump of trees was very thick, and out of there where today there is no road, there was then a road. All of a sudden, on this road came a ghost car, like a black limousine, except that *you could see through it."*

At the same instant, she and her friend Sal saw a German shepherd puppy run alongside their car, with his mouth moving but without any sound, no barking being heard!

"How did the dog disappear?"

"He just ran off the road when the black limousine, a hearse I'd say, pulled out in front of us. There is a cemetery right in back of us, you know."

There still is.

But as Susan and Sal were driving in the opposite direction than the one they had come from, the hearse was going away from the cemetary, not toward it.

"What about the driver of the hearse?"

"Just a shadow. The hearse went alongside our car and then suddenly vanished. The whole episode took maybe seven or eight minutes. We drove back toward Philadelphia very shook up."

Rather than drive on through the strange area of the road, they had decided to turn around and go back the other way.

Now it was our turn to head back to the city. For a while we sat silent, then I asked Sybil Leek to let me know if and when she felt she had something to contribute to the investigation.

"I think if you stayed in this area for a week, you wouldn't know what century you're in," she suddenly said. "I feel very confused . . . almost as if we had entered into another time, and then somebody pushes you back . . . as if they did not want you. This is a very rare situation . . . probably higher intensity of spiritual feeling. . . ."

I then turned to Susan's companion Barbara and asked her about her impressions.

"An apprehensive kind of feeling came over me," she replied. "We were here a week and a half ago again, when we came upon this side of the road, and it was . . . different . . . it felt as if it was not normal. All along this run, as soon as we hit 152, through New Galena, I feel as if I'm *intruding.* . . . as if I don't belong, as though this whole stretch of country were not in existence in my time. I've been out here hundreds of times and always had this odd sensation."

Susan Hardwick and her friends had never attempted to research the past history of the peculiar area of their incidents. But of course I did.

First I contacted the town clerk at Traumbersville, because today that is the nearest town to the area. Specifically I wanted to know whether there ever was a village or a drugstore/bar/restaurant of some sort at the junction of Highway 152 and New Galena Road, not far from the little bridge which is still there. Also, what was the history of the area?

The reply came on March 1, 1968, from the director of the Bucks County Historical Tourist Commission in Fallsington.

> "It is rural farm area now and has been from the beginning. From what I know about this area, and from *Place Names in Bucks County* by George MacReynolds, and Davis' *History of Bucks County,* I know nothing of a dugstore in the area."

There was something else. Susan Hardwick had reported finding some strange holes in the road in the area.

> "They seemed like left from the snow . . . filled with water . . . like a whirlpool. Many times we stopped the car and put our hands into those potholes and *we could not feel the road underneath* them. We—my friends and I—stuck our arms into the holes, and got wet. There was water in them. But when we came back another time, there were no holes. No water. Nothing."

This got me to thinking to search further in George Mac-Reynolds's book. And here is where I found at least a partial explanation for what these people had experienced along New Galena Road.

It appears that back in the 1860s, galena (and lead) ore was discovered in this area and mines were started. Soon there was a mini-gold rush for lead and some silver also, and people in the farm area began driving shafts into the earth to see if there was valuable ore underneath. Those must have been the deep, "bottomless" "potholes" with water in them that Susan and her friends rediscovered—or at least their imprints from the past.

The town of New Galena became a mining center. Mining fever hit the rural population and turned farmers into speculators. By 1874 it was all over, although another attempt at exploiting the mines in the area was made in 1891 and as late as 1932 some work was done to restore railroad tracks to the mines. But it all came to naught. "Today the place is deserted," writes Mac-

Reynolds," a ghost of itself in the boom days of the 60s and 70s."

This explains the strange feeling of not wanting "outsiders" intruding into their own mining bonanza, and it explains the water-filled shafts in the road. What it fails to explain is Jerry's father and the Coke bottles Susan Hardwick and Jerry drank from.

I can only suggest that the intense emotional fervor of a small, backward, rural community suddenly caught up in a mining fever and dreams of great riches, might create a kind of psychic bubble. This aura might continue to exist in a time-space continuum of its own, separate from the outside world . . . except for an occasional, accidental intruder, like Susan and her friends.

RHODE ISLAND

THE ORIGIN OF THE NORSE TOWER

Newport is not only the center of Rhode Island's cultural life and a showplace of fabulous mansions of the very rich, it also has an ancient tower with a mystery of its own.

Situated in Trouro Park, there is a curious round tower with arches on the ground floor, built with rough stones of the kind often used in the early Middle Ages. Until someone decided it was simply the remnant of an old stone mill, it was generally considered to be the work of Vikings who had come to the area. It has been proven they were in Massachusets and Maine.

Similar towers have been built by Norsemen elsewhere, but the similarity did not prevent some latter-day "experts" to discount that origin. They declared it to be nothing more than part of an old stone mill, allegedly built by Governor Benedict Arnold, great-grandfather of the famous traitor, in the seventeenth century. What speaks against this theory is the fact that the tower is a kind of solid fortification. Similar towers are still standing in parts of Ireland.

If you visit this attraction, perhaps your intuition will tell you who built it, after all.

Photos Courtesy of the Newport County Convention and Visitors Bureau

SOUTH CAROLINA

THE GRAY MAN OF PAWLEY'S ISLAND

The sandy beaches of South Carolina's low country are both beautiful and lonely. Not far from George-town, off the coast, lies sprawling Pawley's Island, named after Percival Pawley, who owned it many years ago. Whenever there is approaching danger, such as one of the frequent hurricanes which plague this part of the coast, people report seeing a strange, gray man standing or walking on the dunes. But when they get closer, he just dissolves into thin air. The Gray Man supposedly wants to alert people to the approaching storm. While to some this may be a charming legend, it is hard fact to the actual witnesses who have encountered him.

Businessman William Collins absolutely refused to believe in ghosts, even local ones. During a hurricane watch in 1954, he was walking down the dunes of Pawley's Island to check on the rising surf early in the morning. He thought he was alone, but there, standing on the beach, was a man, looking out to sea. Collins assumed it was one of his neighbors so he called out to the man. But the stranger did not respond in any way. Collins shrugged, and went back into his house.

Photos by Hans Holzer
Drawing by Catherine Buxhoeveden

The weather report assured the islanders that the hurricane had shifted directions and was not likely to hit the area at all. So Collins and his family went to bed that night, no longer worried about the hurricane danger. At five o'clock in the morning Collins was aroused from deep sleep by a heavy pounding on his door. When he opened it, he could feel the house shake from a rising wind, which had, after all, hit the island.

There on his verandah stood a stranger, wearing a gray fishing cap, and a common work shirt and pants—but all of it in gray. Curtly the man told Collins to get off the beach as the storm was heading their way. Quickly, Collins thanked the stranger and ran upstairs to wake his family. When he got down again, just a few minutes later, the stranger had disappeared.

After the storm, Collins made inquiries about the kindly stranger who had warned them, but nobody on the beach had seen him. There was a highway patrolman on duty at the time, but he had not seen any stranger come or leave. Since he was watching the only access to Pawley's Island, the causeway over the marshes, the stranger could not have gone any other way—except into the sea!

Once again, the Gray Man had warned people on the island of impending disaster.

It is generally assumed he is none other than Percival Pawley himself who could not leave his beloved island even in death. Others are convinced he is an unhappy young man who drowned himself in the ocean when he found out that his fiancée had married his best friend. Either way, glimpses of the Gray Man have been recorded here since 1822, and may go back even further.

THE SORORITY HOUSE

The University of Charleston is a magnificently situated set of buildings in antebellum style, set amid flowering trees and shrubbery. It is also an important seat of learning, located in South Carolina's major seaport. The University must have witnessed many an important and dramatic event during its long existence.

Once, when I was speaking at the University, two students took me aside and asked me to investigate their room in one of the old houses serving as a sorority house. It appeared that the room was haunted, and they thought that perhaps it would interest me. The haunted room upstairs seemed unusually cold and clammy, but no ghost made its appearance for me.

When I developed some photographs I took from outside the building, which is called the Lesesne House, a curious thing appeared in the picture. Quite plainly, a female figure in white was visible inside the window of a downstairs room I had just left, *empty*.

Upon further investigation, I discovered that during the Civil War a young woman had hanged herself in that front parlor.

TENNESSEE

WINSTEAD HILL

Winstead Hill is located 840 feet above sea level, two miles from the town of Franklin. It was a natural command and observation post in any battle. Today, the area abounds in wild flowers and trees, giving it a truly rustic and peaceful appearance.

But it was here that one of the bloodiest battles of the Civil War was fought on November 30, 1864. In less than an hour, a total of eighty-five thousand men were killed in this engagement. The Confederate Army of Tennessee charged repeatedly against the poorly-prepared Union earthen "works," the defensive positions protecting them. The Union soldiers were able to pick off the attacking Southerners, which they easily did, making this one of the goriest battles of that unfortunate conflict.

No other battle compares to Winstead Hill in either savagery or loss of life. Five fallen Confederate generals were laid out on the porch of the Carnton House. The battleground has been carefully preserved by the Tennessee Historical Commission.

Photos Courtesy of the Tennessee Historical Commission in Nashville, Tennessee

THE OLD STONE FORT

Located near Manchester, Old Stone Fort Park, which is maintained as a State Archaeological Area by the state of Tennessee, contains the remnants of a fortification built by a people in pre-historic times.

The earth walls are twenty feet thick, and the construction must have been the work of skilled engineers and technicians. The puzzle as to who built this fort remains. Judging from the age of the trees in the immediate area, the fort dates back to well before any white man set foot in this area.

According to Charles Faulkner, who wrote about it in 1968, the site must have been built sometime before 1200 A.D. The civilization and culture of this unknown tribe seems to be more advanced than similar examples of earth works of that period in Mexico and the central United States.

Like many artifacts and "Indian" ruins, these fortifications don't fit into the generally held view of what the native population built or used. They are more closely associated with much earlier civilizations and tend to hint at a European origin, possibly inspired by early arrivals such as the sea people of the Mediterranean. This, of course, does not sit well with conservative archaeologists.

The site is open for inspection daily.

Photographs Courtesy of the Tennessee Historical Commission in Nashville, Tennessee

THE ANCIENT BAT CREEK STONE

Recent findings by the director of the Middletown (New York) Archeological Research Center, Salvatore Michael Trento, and earlier work by the renowned New York University professor, Dr. Cyrus Gordon, have shed new light on an explosive issue that rocked the archeological establishment a few years ago—did sailors from ancient Israel actually land in the United States in 100 A.D.?

The evidence shows that they did, and now archeologists are on the lookout for other, similar gravesites in the hope of discovering additional evidence of this early landing.

The amazing discovery was first made in 1894 when a suspicious "mound," or artificial hill, was reported to the Smithsonian Institute by local residents of Bat Creek, Tennessee, a sleepy little community well inland from the sea. Cyrus Thomas of the Smithsonian, and an excavating party of professional archeologists, arrived on the scene and began opening up the undisturbed site. What the explorers found was truly extraordinary. Among the bones of a number of human beings, there was an oddly-inscribed stone marker which had obviously not been touched since the time it had been buried.

The strange stone slab contained some twelve characters in what the discoverers thought was a Cherokee Indian script. It was probably part of a longer inscription, since some of the stone had crumbled into dust over the years. In his report for the Smithsonian, Cyrus Thomas wrote that he thought he had examined a very old Indian grave. He stressed the fact that the site had been totally undisturbed since the time it had been sealed up. "Beyond question," he wrote, "these are letters of the Cherokee alphabet."

It apparently did not trouble Thomas that the Cherokee alphabet he referred to was not invented until 1821, while the

166

mound, stone, and bones seemed much more ancient. There, the matter remained totally ignored by archeologists and historians, until 1964.

In that year, an enterprising researcher named Henriette Metz discovered that the Smithsonian Institute had mistakingly published the inscription of the stone *upside down!* When she turned it around, the alleged characters of the Cherokee Indian alphabet turned out to be fully-recognizable letters of the ancient Hebrew script. Professor Cyrus Gordon of New York University, a leading archeologist and Near East expert, deciphered the inscription. The letters are the Hebrew characters L Y H W D which mean "for (or from) Judea" or "for the Jews." The style of writing is strikingly similar to writing found in Palestine and dating to the first and second centuries A.D. Professor Gordon felt that "they attest inscriptionally and archeologically to a migration in early Christian times from Judea to our Southeast." He points out that the alphabet on the stone wasn't even deciphered until the late nineteenth century. It couldn't have been the work of the Cherokees.

There are many recent finds of Phoenician and Ibero-Celtic inscribed stones and markers all over the eastern United States. But thus far Bat Creek, Tennessee is the only Jewish gravesite discovered. Its authenticity and age are beyond question. After all, the highly respected Smithsonian Institute excavated it!

The seamen of coastal Palestine and Judea, like their Phoenician neighbors, were forever roaming the oceans in search of new trade partners. Apparently one of their ships somehow went further and wound up in America. When they could not return to their far-off homeland, they let the world know who they were and where they had come from. Thus, the Bat Creek Hebrew stone stands as a significant marker of a daring people's ancient voyage to these shores.

The stone itself is in the Smithsonian Institute in Washington, D.C. Attacks upon its authenticity have been made over the years, mainly by people who have never examined it or the circumstances of its discovery.

VERMONT

A SUBTERRANEAN CHAMBER AT WESTMINSTER

Vermont, along with parts of New Hampshire and Massachusetts, was touched upon by many people from across the sea. These adventurers either sailed here in search of new land, or were driven here by winds. New England is dotted with genuine artifacts of ancient origin.

The chamber in the woods of Westminster is similar to a chamber at Mystery Hill in Salem, New Hampshire and to such chambers connected with Ibero-Celtic and Celtic centers in Europe and the Mediterranean area, dating between 3000 and 1500 B.C.

The subterranean chamber at Westminster is part of a network of temple ruins left in New England, bearing unmistakable signs of having been built by European arrivals in the pre-Christian era. The chambers were used as so-called oracle chambers where priests consulted their gods. Roughly hewn, but carefully constructed, they could not possibly have been the work of native Indians. In addition, radiocarbon 14 dating has established their age.

Photo by Lauren Raine

VIRGINIA

THE NATURAL BRIDGE

The ancients had their seven wonders, which included such man-made monuments as the Colossus of Rhodes and the Pyramids.

More recent wonders might include the Eiffel Tower and the Empire State Building. But then there are the natural wonders of the world, and the Natural Bridge near Lexington is certainly one of them.

The Natural Bridge towers 215 feet above the road, and is ninety feet long. Nature carved the arch out of rock by way of a mountain stream. At one time Thomas Jefferson owned the site, and built a cabin nearby to accommodate visitors, including George Washington, who had come to survey the arch. General Washington by the way had been a surveyor by trade before the Revolutionary War caught up with him.

Today, the Natural Bridge Village has a hotel, simply called The Inn, as well as those cottages started by Jefferson.

Photo Courtesy of the Virginia Division of Tourism

WESTOVER

One of the most famous American mansions is Westover, built in 1730 by Col. William Byrd II, a member of the Virginia aristocracy. The style is that of the Palladian mansions of Europe.

Byrd was a wealthy planter who wanted a house that could rival the Greathouses of England and Ireland. He chose a spot two miles above the James River, with a view toward the sailing ships that lay at anchor there. Byrd died during the Revolutionary War and he is buried there in the walled boxwood garden. While the house itself can be visited only with permission of the owners, the gardens are open to the public at certain times.

It isn't the splendor of the mansion alone that draws visitors. Col. Byrd went to London with his beautiful daughter Evelyn in 1717 to help celebrate the coronation of King George I. Evelyn remained in England to be educated when her father returned to Virginia. Soon he received news that young Evelyn had fallen in love with Charles Mordaunt, the grandson of the Earl of Peterborough. He was an eligible man except for one, important fact— he was an ardent Roman Catholic, and Evelyn's father an equally ardent Protestant. It would never do, so Colonel Byrd ordered his daughter to return home immediately.

Evelyn had no choice but to obey. The moment she set foot again at Westover, she went into isolation. She was suffering from a broken heart, and refused to receive any potential suitor, showing her father and family the cold shoulder.

Evelyn became more and more frail and before long had to be confined to her bed. Sure she was going to die, Evelyn spoke to her close friend, Anne Harrison, telling her of her premonition. But she assured Anne that she would stay in contact even after her death. A few weeks later, Evelyn passed away.

The following spring, after everyone had somewhat gotten

Photos Courtesy of the Virginia Division of Tourism

over the shock of Evelyn's untimely passing, Anne Harrison was walking in the gardens when she saw her old friend Evelyn standing in front of her, wearing a brilliant white gown and smiling at her. The apparition seemed younger than the age of twenty-nine which Evelyn had reached at the time of her death.

Since then, others have encountered the lovely wraith at Westover. A neighbor saw her in the 1960s coming out of the front gate. Then the apparition sank into the ground before her eyes!

A house guest of a neighbor saw her in the garden one moonlit night, and reported that Evelyn waved at her.

I have not been able to bring a competent medium to Westover to release Evelyn. The present owners cannot seem to come to terms with the tragedy of the past, but surely it is time to reconcile Colonel Byrd and his lovely daughter.

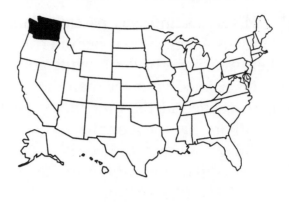

WASHINGTON

GINKO PETRIFIED FOREST

Ellensburg, Washington is best known as the center of the apple-growing business, but it also has another attraction.

The Petrified Forest at Ginko State Park shows many examples of pre-historic trees that have been preserved for thirteen million years. Groves of trees were sacred sites in pre-historic times, and this spot may well have had that connotation also.

The earliest inhabitants of this region were people of the Stone Age. Their religion was truly animistic, with the sun, moon and stars representing gods. Natural objects, such as trees had special significance, because they "reached into the sky" to touch the realm of the gods. Thus, ancient sanctuaries were often found in the woods, among a cluster of tall trees. What is remarkable about this site is that we get a glimpse of an actual example of such "tree sanctuaries," even if petrified.

Photo Courtesy of Steve Wang, Washington State Parks and Recreation Commission

THE SUQUAMISH OLD-MAN HOUSE SITE

Across Puget Sound from the city of Seattle lies a spot on the shore where once stood the remarkable house of Chief Seattle.

The house, nine hundred feet long, was a major center for native Americans in the first half of the nineteenth century. Chief Seattle was considered in his time a wise leader. He was a powerful and respected chief, who headed the Indian Confederation in the Pacific Northwest in the nineteenth century. Far from going on the warpath against the ever-encroaching white settlers, he found a way to live with them and often prevented bloody encounters between his people and the whites.

The chief's "house" was far more than a private residence. It was actually the community meeting house, a long and narrow wooden building, where as many as one hundred people could sit down and talk. It served as a kind of primitive parliament for his people, and also as a place where negotiations with the white settlers took place.

The house is no more, but the site where it once stood is still considered sacred ground by many native Americans.

Photo Courtesy of Steve Wang, Washington State Parks and Recreation Commission

WEST VIRGINIA

Created during the Civil War when some of the people of Virginia preferred to stay with the Union, West Virginia is full of wilderness and primitive conditions. But it also boasts some fascinating and mysterious places where a curious traveller might pick up vibrations from the past, those spent emotions that never quite went away.

THE JEFFERSON COUNTY COURTHOUSE

In 1859 abolitionist John Brown stood trial in the Jefferson County Courthouse in Charles Town (not to be confused with Charleston, also in West Virginia) for his raid on Harper's Ferry. Brown was found guilty of treason and was hung. The site of his gallows can be seen and if you are psychic enough, perhaps you may feel something.

LOST RIVER STATE PARK

In the early part of the nineteenth century, Lost River State Park was known as Lee's White Sulphur Springs, and it was a well-frequented health spa. The river which gave this waterway its peculiar name, disappears—is lost—under a mountain and comes out on the other side where it has a different name—Cacapon River. The Lee who ran the resort was Harry Lee, father of General Robert E. Lee. The cabin Harry Lee built for himself can still be visited.

BLENNERHASSET ISLAND

Situated in the Ohio River due south of the city of Parkersburg, this island was absolute wilderness back in 1805. That was when Aaron Burr, Vice President of the United States, hatched a plot to establish an independent empire in the American southwest. Burr was caught and tried for treason and fled for his life to France. Napoleon, ever sympathetic to unusual empire builders, gave him asylum and some support.

Burr had met a wealthy Irishman named Harman Blennerhasset here and persuaded him to join and help finance his aborted cause. Blennerhasset built himself a stately mansion on the island. He was never brought to trial, although he was financially ruined when the plot failed. A few broken stones is all that remains of his original mansion, but there are later buildings on the island. It is worth a visit, if only to wonder what mysterious attraction the plot had for a well-established, wealthy man.

Photo by David Fattaleh, Courtesy of the Division of Tourism and Parks, State of West Virginia

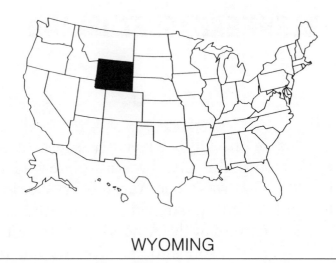

WYOMING

DEVIL'S TOWER

When Captain W. F. Reynolds and his party reached this spot in 1859, they were the first white men to see this incredible rock rising 1280 feet above the Belle Fourche River. Located near Sundance, the butte is actually an 865-foot monolith formed by molten lava some fifty million years ago.

The Indians referred to it as Bad God's Tower or sometimes as Grizzly Bear Lodge, because a legend has it that the rock was raised to save seven young Indian girls from a grizzly bear. In 1875 Richard I. Dodge of the U.S. Geological Survey named it Devil's Tower. In 1893 local ranchers fashioned a wooden ladder on its side, so that people can actually ascend it. In 1906 this tower became the first National Monument in the United States.

Most movie-goers will recognize it as the spot where extra-terrestrials finally met up with Richard Dreyfus and his fellow actors in *Close Encounters of the Third Kind.*

The site is north of Sundance in Crook County, in the north-eastern corner of the state of Wyoming.

Photo Courtesy of the Wyoming State Museum

THE MEDICINE WHEEL AT BIG HORN

Near Big Horn, there is an almost perfect circle of stones sunk into the ground. The circle is seventy feet in diameter with twenty-eight spokes radiating from a central stone cairn, and six stone cairns placed around the circle itself, all facing the rising sun.

The Wheel was first discovered by white men in the 1880s. Despite the fact that the Sheepeater Indians claim they built it, and may in fact have used the giant wheel in ceremonies of their own, the Medicine Wheel is not theirs at all. It is a very accurate observatory very much like those found in England and other Celtic sites in the United States.

Every June 21, the summer solstice, two of the stone cairns on the western side of the Wheel mark the exact sunrise and sunset on that day. The Wheel also gives exact readings in respect to the position of certain stars, such as Sirius, Rigel in Orion, and Aldebaran in Taurus. All of which points to a much older origin for the Medicine Wheel, and others like it, going back ten thousand years.

The people who built this observatory must then be the "cousins" of those who left Europe and came to North America between 3000 and 1500 B.C. and built New Hampshire's Mystery Hill and other pre-Columbian monuments. North American "Indians" are very likely descendants of migrating tribes who came from Mongolia and the Asian steppes over the Bering Sea landbridge. They settled in lands already discovered by a race of Ibero-Celtic people.